God is Never Late...

A GREAT wave of inspired spiri   ıg
across the English-speaking world, producing fundamental
changes in our understanding of ourselves and the universe in
which we exist.

God Is Never Late, an extraordinary collection of channelled
commentaries given to Ian Graham by a spiritual entity calling
himself 'White Bull' now enters on the crest of this wave. 'This
book has come into being through grace and magic,' says the
author. 'As White Bull might have said, "God's fingerprints are
all over it" '.

Succinct, ever terse in places, and spiced with engaging flashes
of humour, these writings lead us with an often maverick
originality into new dimensions of insight and illumination —
particularly on questions of karma, human sexuality and our
relationship with other worlds and other lives.

White Bull also addresses a wide array of pressing contemporary global issues — from AIDS and the 'Greenhouse Effect' to
the conflict between conventional and complementary medicine
and the reasons for the recent worldwide increase in natural
disasters.

At another level the book offers answers to some acutely
personal questions: 'Why am I here?...' 'Why did I choose my
family?...' 'How can I know what information to trust?...' 'Why
does the spiritual path have to be so difficult at times?

Overall, however, the most striking and constant feature of the
book is the deep love, compassion, reassurance and comfort
which it offers page by page to those already searching
diligently for ultimate spiritual truths. To read it is to feel
uplifted, heartened and spiritually refreshed. Already published
to acclaim in Germany and The Netherlands, *God Is Never Late*
appears to be destined to take its own very high place
internationally among outstanding modern spiritual writings.

This book is dedicated with fondest love and infinite gratitude

To the memory of my Father,
David Graham

and

To my Mother,
Sheila Graham

GOD IS NEVER LATE...

but never early either!

*Reassurance for humanity
from another dimension*

IAN GRAHAM
with
White Bull

TAGMAN

www.tagman-press.com
London, Sydney, Los Angeles

GOD IS NEVER LATE...

First published in English in Great Britain in the year 2000 by
The Tagman Press, an imprint of Tagman Worldwide Ltd,

2 Elmdon Court, St. Leonards Road, Norwich NR1 4JP, UK.,
1888 Century Park East, Suite 1900, Los Angeles CA 90067-1702, USA.,
31 Denham Street, Bondi, NSW 2026, Australia.
e-mail:editorial@tagman-press.com

First published in Dutch by Uitgeverij Ankh-Hermes bv, Deventer,
The Netherlands in 1999 as:
GOD IS NOOIT TE LAAT (MAAR OOK NOOIT TE VROEG)

The right of Ian Graham to be identified as the author of this work has been
asserted by him in accordance with the Copyright,
Designs and Patents Act 1988

ISBN: 1-903571-01-4

A CIP catalogue record for this book is available from
The British library

Edited by Lucy Grey & Hazel Cripps
Cover design by Barnaby Phillips
Typeset in Times New Roman by G. Malcolm Mitchell
Printed by MFP Design and Print, Manchester M32 0JT, UK

TAGMAN

www.tagman-press.com
London, Sydney, Los Angeles

CONTENTS

CONTENTS

FOREWORD

BY

Princess Irene of The Netherlands

I MET White Bull several years ago. Someone had advised me to go and meet him. I am somewhat reluctant about mediums; I prefer a person to person conversation, but looking deep into my heart I found it was right to go. Driving over to my first rendez-vous I asked for a sign to confirm it was really all right to go and there, to my left just over the farmhouse where White Bull would talk through Ian Graham, a huge rainbow appeared. Since then a rainbow has appeared whenever something really important was about to happen to me and I felt either nervous or uncertain about it. I get the feeling this is White Bull telling me everything is all right and I should celebrate.

I have come to love this dear friend, who never tells you what will happen next but is always there with you, to make you feel special and loved. This old soul has chosen to be near humans with compassion, truth and encouragement in this time of great change, to give those of us who are willing to listen a broader perspective, not only on our personal lives but also on the world we live in and the laws of nature ruling our universe.

He fills us with love and understanding. 'All is perfect. You are perfect' is what he will say over and over again, telling us not to try to become the perfect person we want to be, but to relax into who we are, in every stage of our lives on our own personal road towards our own personal goal — that road we chose to walk following our own truths, to learn our own personal lessons.

About this road White Bull says 'I cannot promise you it will be without pain, just as for the flower bud to open, the membrane which has protected it must die; any web of illusion, any false persona, any belief in separation must fall away so that your beauty and purpose can be revealed and your fragrant benediction can be released into the world. And you know, Dear Ones, if you had the ears to hear and you put your ear to a rosebud, you would hear its cries of pain as it opens to reveal its beauty.'

He does not say we can cuddle up and be happy with ourselves; he certainly warns us about comfort and righteousness, but then again he leaves it to each one of us to do what we feel we need to do. After a talk with White Bull I feel blessed and seen and filled up with his unconditional love, so much so that I can pass it on to others.

Ian Graham has dedicated his life to White Bull in his role as the instrument, meanwhile spreading his very own joyous love around him in his daily life. By writing this book he has chosen to become more visible himself, to enable White Bull's universal messages to spread to a greater public at a time when we all need encouragement to heal the Earth through healing ourselves.

'You think nothing of referring to your rain forests as the lungs of the Earth Mother, to your rivers as the veins, but you can take it much further than that if you understand really how She is reflecting back to you the state of health of the collective human consciousness.'

May this book touch many who seek to live in harmony with the Earth, themselves and others.

INTRODUCTION

How I met White Bull

WHEN THE NAME WHITE BULL first dropped into my head during a meditation nearly seventeen years ago I was immediately reminded of my very first record played on my new Dansette, a gift for my seventh birthday. For days afterwards Tommy Steele's rendition of 'A Little White Bull' played itself incessantly in my head.

I was twenty-nine, and true to form my Saturn Return; the planetary transit which portends dramatic change, was about to turn my life really upside down. A few weeks later I heard about the phenomenon of channelling from a friend for the first time. 'Be careful, you are being conned. This sort of thing can't happen' was my first reaction. A week later I was having my first reading from a dis-incarnate being. After my third reading 'Teacher', as this entity was called invited me to join his group. Soon after I found myself the new boy in a development circle led by 'Teacher', that had already been going for eighteen months. I was not nervous, just sceptical, very sceptical.

The first thing we did that evening was to meditate and as soon as I closed my eyes I found myself in an Indian encampment. 'How clichéd' I thought to myself. 'Teacher's' voice interrupted my thoughts to give me a guided tour of this camp, as if he were in there with me. 'That's me, that's the wife, that's my tepee third from the left,' and so on. The 'camera' inside my head panned round and I saw a big Indian standing under a tree holding his horse. 'And that one over there, he's my friend White Bull and he's going to work with you.' You could have knocked me down with one of his white feathers!

Three weeks later, while meditating, I got the sensation of my hands growing and my body filling out (probably to my present proportions: I was still smoking so this is seventeen years and forty pounds ago!) I felt my face changing too. I was developing a facial bone structure to die for — high cheek bones and a firm jaw — just like the photos of Indians I had seen in books. And then, beyond my control a voice boomed out 'I am White Bull'. My fate was sealed.

'This will impress them when someone asks me what I do', I thought, but when the umpteenth person's eyes glazed over I gave up telling. It seemed so much more glamourous than all the other dead end jobs I had been doing since I left my expensive public school in Edinburgh. While my classmates had been advancing through the ranks of their merchant banks and lawyers offices, I was still 'searching' for what I wanted to do with my life. How I used to dread the question 'What are you doing with yourself nowadays, Graham?'

With a staunch Church of Scotland missionary background and the consequent programming to serve coursing through my veins I guess avocation to help and heal was unavoidable, but why this one in particular that would place me beyond the fringes of what was socially acceptable in my society, especially within my own family, and press every sceptical button in me to boot? Many a tantrum followed that initial meeting with White Bull and for the first two years that I was channelling for others I did not even believe in what I was doing, although I could see it was helping them. But deep down I knew he had me over a barrel. I could only surrender and my search was over.

Nevertheless during the last seventeen years I have often felt that I was completely the wrong person to be doing a job like this and in my more rebellious moments I have continued to ask myself, as I have been asked by countless others also, 'Why did White Bull choose you?' Why me indeed? Is it my karma? Did White Bull and I draw straws in the spirit world to decide who would return to Earth to be the instrument? Did White Bull choose me because my strict upbringing taught me to do as I was told and therefore I would not resist? As my friends will testify, at such moments the worst thing to say to me is: 'Well you chose it!' It is the worst thing to say probably because my ego is not yet ready to hear the truth, that indeed my soul chose this task before I incarnated. 'So much for free will!' my ego retaliates.

My early resolve that nobody would have reason to call me a

charlatan led me to find out as much as I could about channelling. I learned that far from being merely a New Age phenomenon, it has been practiced for centuries in many different cultures in the name of oracles, shamans, witch doctors, and prophets and that many indigenous communities and tribes have always had access to a higher wisdom speaking through such a medium. Still today the State Oracle of Tibet, the spirit of Nechung speaking through a human instrument, guides the Tibetan leaders in exile. And in my opinion there is ample evidence in the Bible that Jesus saw himself as a channel when he said: 'It is not I who does the work but my Father in Heaven who sent me'. Jesus' words provide a simple explanation for me of one of the prime requisites for becoming a channel which is the capacity to put the self or the ego on one side.

I quickly realised also that discovering I was a channel was not a sign of having 'arrived' but a point of departure, for such a task cannot, I believe, be successfully carried out without rigorous attention being paid to ones 'stuff', especially the rooting out of prejudices which if they remain unconscious may colour the message. I also made a personal decision not to read any other channelled or similar books so that I had the reassurance that what came through me was not a regurgitation of what I had read even if, as I have often discovered, White Bull's wisdom dovetails with that of other sources. My meeting with White Bull began a journey of self-healing and discovery that continues to this day and which I hope leaves me a purer channel with each little step I take.

And so another frequently asked question arises — who, or what, is White Bull? Is he a separate entity or is he a sub-personality of mine? Or is he wholly or part of my higher self, whatever that is? I have always sympathised with anyone sitting opposite me who, watching me channel, thinks to themselves, 'This isn't White Bull; it must be Ian' because in a similar situation I might feel the same. I can offer no proof but I do know that in my own experience when I close my eyes at the beginning of a trance session I definitely feel an energy coming into my body, like an electrical current and, according to some trusted friends, my demeanour changes to one rather more dignified and poised than my normal state of being. Those with clairvoyant vision report a lot of activity in my aura at the same time. It is while all this is happening that I am in the process of surrendering to White Bull — though not before I know for sure that it is him.

When he speaks there is a slight change in the modulation of my voice, perhaps merely to reassure the listener that another being is there. The difference is much less than in the early days when probably my ego needed to have that difference to reassure me that a separate entity was present. White Bull is more articulate than I am normally; there are no 'ums' and 'errs' in his conversation for he does not have to think what to say! He is also much wittier than I am which my ego used to have a particularly hard time handling. And when he leaves my body, it is like waking up knowing that you have had a dream but you are unable to remember the details.

But these explanations could still provide a rationalist or a psychologist with sufficient ammunition to debunk what is happening and to pathologise me. While I remain in general a sceptic I am happy to have found a security within myself to allow people to believe what they like about who or what White Bull is. What is beyond doubt is that his presence is accompanied by a quality of love that could not be faked. And if someone cannot feel it, there is no point in trying to prove otherwise. As White Bull says, there is no point in trying to prove to someone without a sense of smell that the roses in your garden have a beautiful perfume. You either have that sense or not.

Happily there are enough people who have that sense for there to be a global network of White Bull's friends. Sometimes they meet one another in strange ways; fellow passengers stranded in foreign airports and once the only two Europeans flying on a domestic flight in Japan found themselves sitting next to each other and discovered they had a mutual friend in White Bull. In New Zealand there is a valley named after him and in Belgium an artists' management company and even a record label bear his name.

His influence extends to other areas of the performing arts. An American film director discusses the themes for his films with him and he has contributed to at least one ballet production at the Opera in Paris by one of the world's greatest choreographers.

The White Bull 'gang' comes from all walks of life; thousands of people in the last seventeen years have had the highest and deepest in them touched by his great love, warmth and humour, for he will never allow anyone to take themselves too seriously for too long, least of all himself. For some their relationship with him is confined to their conversations with him. For others he is a frequent guest in their lives. 'I am delighted to tell you that from now on you are stuck with me' are often his parting words. He is felt as a loving presence by many as he makes his 'house calls' and often will leave a visiting card of a white feather.

One such occasion arose when White Bull invited himself as an occasional holiday companion for a depressed client who was going to the Greek Islands. He told this man that he would make his presence known by a pile of white feathers. On the first island he visited the man was disturbed as he sunbathed on the beach by a strange noise and looked up to see a white goose walking towards him. When the goose was near him it began to pull some feathers out of its breast and deposited a small pile of them beside the man's towel. At the next island he was similarly disturbed, but this time it was a white duck which did the same thing!

White Bull is also not averse to playing Cupid. I have recently been a witness for the third time at a marriage where White Bull made the initial introduction.

Most recently a Dutch client who is the captain of a Boeing 747 was flying at 30,000 feet over the Persian Gulf when he heard a voice on his cockpit radio asking 'Is that Chris?' 'Yes' he replied, 'who is that?' 'A friend of White Bull' came the reply from the cockpit of another KLM plane flying 300 miles behind.

Sometimes press publicity is less than respectful. A few years ago a tongue-in-cheek article about White Bull and myself appeared in *Tatler* magazine. The article began with the words 'Hackett jacket and country cord wearer, Ian Graham...' — were that I could afford a Hackett Jacket! — and concluded by saying in addition that some people were '...drawn merely to the spectacle of a quintessentially English gentleman speaking with an American Indian accent'.

Such reactions make my hackles rise less now than they did then. It was okay for me to be sceptical about channelling but then it still hurt

13

when somebody else was sceptical about it. After all, I knew I wasn't a charlatan.

Nevertheless I have every sympathy with anyone who may be sitting opposite me in a trance, listening to White Bull who thinks this is Ian really, not some spirit. For to the reasoning, analytical mind — and as a Virgo I know all about that — it is all too easy to come to that conclusion.

I accept that for as long as I am working as a channeller there will always remain for some people that question mark above my work which says: 'is it Ian or is it White Bull?' Happily, there are many, people including some who I believe to be infinitely more evolved than myself, who are convinced by their personal experience of his existence.

There are some who believe that White Bull is a part of me or that I am the reincarnation of White Bull. Others still do not care either way and are simply helped by the message. White Bull, who of course is without ego, has no interest at all in proving his existence or the validity of his message. Let love speak for itself, he will say, and will always encourage the listener to feel within themselves if what he is saying is true for them.

Today White Bull — or Mr Bull, W.B., or, White Stuff to call him by some of his pet names — has lodged himself in the hearts and minds of many people through his loving counsel and gentle humour. For over thirty weeks of the year I travel Northern Europe giving private sessions, and lecturing to groups on channelling and associated topics, each time gaining more friends, for myself as well as White Bull. Grace — perhaps another name for White Bull — has seen to it that I have never had to lift a finger to make any of it happen. Now I am glad, even honoured, to be known as his Instrument.

1

GREETINGS FROM
WHITE BULL

HELLO MY friends and welcome. I am White Bull and we bring you a warm and very loving greeting. I am delighted to have this opportunity to fulfil my greatest desire which is to serve you, to bring you, through my words, to a place of deeper peace, greater clarity and better understanding. More than that I hope that my teachings will serve the purpose of injecting a little oil into the wheels of your life, that your journey in life can be a more comfortable and a more beautiful one, and so liberate you from constraint upon your well being.

As such it is my desire that my words relate to your life now, and how now, which is the moment of creation, you can transform your human existence into a celebration of all that is good, that is God. I do not want you to use my teachings to prepare for a future that others may have told you is coming, but to create the future which is the highest you can imagine.

I want you to know also that I serve you on behalf of the Highest in you and I hope you will find the truth of that in the resonance that you feel in the deepest part of you as you read my words. As such the greatest compliment that you can pay me is to say: 'Well of course I knew it all already!'

I must also explain to you who 'we' are for I could not bring you these teachings on my own. Allow me then to tell you a little story.

Once upon a time there was a little band of Indians who used to go out riding together. One day however the youngest amongst them decided to go out on his own and test himself against the challenges of life 'out there'. Unknown to him his friends followed him, shadowing his every step until he made the decision to explore the bottom of the ravine. They watched him as he easily found a way to the floor of the ravine and they watched him as he began the journey up again. But he took a different path to come up and when he was nearly at the top he found himself stuck on a ledge. His friends watched him lovingly as he pondered the choices. They were so close to each other that they could communicate telepathically to him not to go down to the bottom again even though he would have been more comfortable there, but instead to wait. His friends, who were always prepared for every eventuality chose the one amongst them who was closest to him to be lowered down on the end of a rope so that he could help the one who was stuck; those who remained, who as luck would have it were the strongest, could then help to bring them to the top.

Well, Dear Ones, I am the one who is dangling at the end of the rope! And believe me, holding the rope, are dear friends of mine, and yours, in the world of light who, like me, long to raise you up that you may find the path of truth.

2

YOUR PERFECT
TIMING

DEAR ONES, you marvel that your scientists can send a rocket to the moon and bring it back on time. But is it not even more remarkable that you have travelled for centuries in many different physical bodies and that now you have arrived back here on Earth, on time!

For many of you your presence now in a human form arises from a commitment made aeons ago to be alive at this all important moment in your planet's history. And a part of that commitment made all that time ago was to agree to experience in the intervening period everything necessary to equip you for the task that now awaits you.

Now at that time, at the beginning of this cycle of incarnations, you agreed to embrace in each life a dominant factor or lesson to prepare you for your work in this incarnation. Perhaps you learned in one lifetime the lessons of sacrifice and the errors of that way; in another about devotion to a cause; in yet another to learn about human relationships and community. In every one of them you have had lessons in the use of power. The result is that in all of these lives not one area of human experience has been left unchallenged.

But you have found in this lifetime, choosing to be born in the civilisation of which you are a part, that every aspect of your being has been touched already, your spiritual life, your creative life, your emotional life and more. You may feel that you have had several lifetimes' worth of pain already in this life. This chapter of your present physical embodiment has needed to be a concentration, a weaving together into one knot, of all of the strands from the past so that in the impulse to unravel it all, you reconnect with the vision which brought you into this body in the first place.

We see so many of you working tirelessly on yourselves in order to heal the wounds of your past and how discouraged you become when what you thought was healed raises its ugly head again. The struggle seems never ending. It is like travelling on a mountain railway; you are in a dark tunnel then suddenly emerge into the daylight, but before your eyes have had a chance to adjust to the light so that you can take in the beautiful view you are back in the tunnel. Don't be discouraged. Remember, you are preparing for something immense; that is not accomplished in days. Every tunnel is necessary to take you higher, even to the summit of human consciousness. Consider too that those tunnels are in fact the safest place to be, maybe even the darker the better, for it is only when you are in a tunnel so dark that you cannot see your nose in front of your face that you have to rely upon God alone. If there were even a faint shadow you would rely upon that first to lead you out. You will save yourself so much energy if instead of thrashing around in your pain for an understanding to hold on to, you could just give yourself to God's loving embrace, as you might sink into a hot bath or your favourite armchair after a hard day's work.

We know too how frustrating it is for you when you look around at those who appear to have no interest in self-growth but have no problems in manifesting those things that you are working towards. Their lives seem so easy by comparison. The reason why life appears so easy for them is none of your business. The reason why your path does not bring you what you want in your life is not because there is any injustice in Divine Law for indeed you can have all that you want at every level. But you have chosen at the level of your Higher Self to follow a path where you will manifest your needs through Divine Law and not by your will power.

Be sure that you are not confusing the spiritual path with the path of self-healing which may be more psychological in nature. The latter will not necessarily be enough to bring you what you want for it deals with the mind and the heart only to the extent that wounds from the past are healed. It is the preparing of the soil in your garden, the clearing away of the stones and weeds. The spiritual path is the sowing of the seeds and the diligent, disciplined nurturing of those seeds so that there may come an abundant harvest, your self-realisation, contained within which will be the fulfilment of all your needs, but not always your desires. The spiritual path is your task alone; no one, and no book, can do it for you.

You will of course have moments, some longer than others, when you will feel like throwing it all in and leading a normal life once again, but I promise you that even in those crisis moments you are drawing nearer and nearer to the breakthrough that you long for. Whatever lack of results there may appear to be we know that you are doing your best. Do not judge yourself, ever, or feel that you are failing. Just look into your heart and remind yourself of what you know is the intention engraved upon your heart and from that take courage. And of course do not forget to congratulate yourself on your excellent timing, not just for arriving in your present physical body so punctually, but also for allowing your path to unfold as it is doing now. Trust that as your life unfolds everything will happen at the perfect time. Know without a doubt that God is never late but accept that He is never early either.

3

THE NEW
MILLENNIUM

DEAREST FRIENDS, when you read this many of the predictions for the period you have just lived through will not have happened. Certainly not those which prophesied an apocalyptic scenario. I trust therefore that you are breathing freely and are looking forward with optimism to the future.

For those of you who mark the passing of time by the Christian calendar and for whom the year represents an important birthday, what matters most is not any numeric significance, but that it has focussed your attention upon the life and example of the great teacher and healer, Jesus of Nazareth. As such, when so many thoughts and prayers are being directed towards Him, how can the light of the Christ which he so perfectly embodied not draw very close to you all? How can the same spirit not grow in you? How can you not draw fresh inspiration from His example and renew your intent to follow in His way? And in His closeness, as in the closeness to you now of so many great souls, is found the reassurance that it is safe to let go of the past, to live in the now without fear of the future.

It is customary for many of you to make special resolutions at the beginning of each new year, promises to yourself that you will not do something anymore or that you will begin a new and positive habit, so we rejoice when we observe how many of you are joining in a collective resolution to create a better world.

But when you have shared your intent with that collective resolution or if you have made one in the privacy of your own heart, for it to make any lasting difference in your world there needs to be at the basis of it an unequivocal resolve to forgive; to forgive everyone in your past for every hurt, real or imagined. And as entering into this New Millennium will not see an immediate end to all of the human behaviour that so offends your sensibilities, so you must be willing from now on to forgive immediately any seeming wrong-doing by anyone towards any part of Divine creation.

Not to forgive is no less a denial of the Christ than that of your brother, the disciple Peter when he denied three times any knowledge of his Master. Not to forgive is to perpetuate a world of duality where notions of good and bad, right and wrong thrive and thus imprison the fragile egos of those who are enthralled by material reality alone. The world that you hope to create in the coming Millennium by the fruits of your resolutions cannot come to pass if you hold any resentments towards others or feel guilt towards yourself. Nor can it come if the scales of justice are tipped either way but only when they are in perfect balance.

Remember, forgiveness is not an attitude to ease your conscience or erase the effect of 'wrong' having been done; rather it is to dissolve attachment to a belief in 'wrong' and liberate from duality.

By forgiving instead of judging or feeling wronged you not only express a trust in the perfection of Divine justice but you also begin to raise your consciousness to a level that the light which shines from you makes it harder for anyone to act or speak in your company in a way that could offend you.

Through forgiveness some part of you is reminded of where you once stood on the evolutionary journey, perhaps in lifetimes that you cannot remember or even incidents in your present life, and that you have transcended the ignorance that led you then to harm another. From such a realisation can spring the qualities of humility and thankfulness for the Grace that has helped you to transcend, qualities essential for your Ascension.

It is as you forgive everything and everyone from your past that your heart can finally open to experience true thankfulness for what is past, for you will then understand the perfection of the path that you have come; you will then understand truly the words 'As God is for you, what can be against you?'

Dear Ones, can you imagine a more beautiful gift to take into the world at the beginning of a New Millennium? What reassurance you can bring to those who live in fear by the spirit of thankfulness that radiates from you! What freedom you can bring to them by the stream of consciousness that flows ceaselessly around you through you and which says 'You are forgiven!' If only you could see, as I can, the countless human beings who in their souls long to hear those words coming from you who truly speaks with authority of the Christ. Then they will in that instant cease all those unloving actions that hurt and destroy any part of Divine creation and through which they express their longing for love.

Whatever your New Millennium resolution is, whether it is for something in your own life or on behalf of mankind, you will find it so much easier to keep and make it work by making first the resolution to forgive. And if the worst comes to the worst and you cannot keep it you will at least find it a lot easier to forgive yourself.

Dearest friends, a Happy New Millennium to you all.

4

YOUR
FLOWERING

THINK OF your garden in Spring. The warmth of the sun begins to draw to the surface the new growth. But before the shoots can appear above the surface the growth must first take place in the darkness of the soil. When the seed first germinates the shoot is drawn in a direction that it cannot resist but in such darkness it has no points of reference to tell it where it is. Then there comes that magical moment when it pushes its way through the surface; then it not only sees the sun that has been drawing it upwards but it finds that it is not alone, that there are others like it who have also journeyed in the darkness. But seeing the light is not the end of the journey, for it must now test its strength against the elements until it grows strong enough so that nothing can harm it until the moment when the membrane that protects the bud is ready to break and the flowering can take place.

Your journey, from the time you left the spirit world to enter into your physical body up to this moment now, and perhaps even beyond now, is like the journey of this plant. The time spent growing in the darkness is the time when you could not know why you were here on Earth, you did not know where you were going and maybe were only unconsciously aware of a force drawing you forward. You felt lonely and different but did not know why and certainly could not imagine that there were others like you. And then came the moment of breakthrough, when you made your first contact with something or someone of a spiritual nature. You saw the light and you thought to yourself I've arrived! I've come home! You met others who were like you and also on the same journey. But as you found out you were not really yet home, you had not said goodbye to your pain because the journey upwards brings its own trials and tribulations. And for many of you that journey still goes on.

Never doubt, that the moment of flowering, the moment of self-realisation, of your fullest potential being realised is coming, must come, for how can a flower resist opening to the warmth of the sun? You do not need to know when, for the flowering always takes place in God's time, in the fullness of time. And I cannot promise you that it will be without pain as for the bud to open the membrane which has protected it must die; any web of illusion, any false persona, any belief in separation must fall away so that your beauty can be revealed and your fragrant benediction can be released into the world.

And you know, Dear Ones, if you had the ears to hear and you put your ear to a rose bud you would also hear its cries of pain as it opens to reveal its beauty.

5

AWAKENING
THE CHRIST

How can I awaken the Christ in me?

BY LOOKING for It in others, for it takes One to see One. And for that you have to acknowledge the presence of the Christ in others which is an important first step.

It follows that you will then want to apply yourself to breaking the habit of judging people by their appearances or wounded behavioural patterns — the second important step.

When you have acknowledged that the Christ is in all and that therefore all are essentially perfect you can start training yourself to look upon all, even those whose surface selves you do not like, with infinite compassion, as a Christ would; you will see also that they are in your life as your teachers, as Christ is.

If you are in a difficult relationship with someone, do not imprison them with your thought forms of their imperfections. Instead next time you speak to them imagine you are speaking to the Christ in them; by doing so you will connect with that level in them and will begin to draw it to the surface, thus liberating them from their old patterns of behaviour. You will also liberate your own heart from the fears that give rise to the need to judge another.

This is how Jesus healed. When He healed the blind man, of course Jesus saw with his physical eye that the man was blind, but when He said to him: 'Open your eyes and see!' He was speaking to the perfect being, the Christ, in that man that He could also perceive. The perfect in the blind man responded to the call and came forth and he was blind no more.

Jesus of course had the added benefit of absolute faith and this was conveyed in his words in such a way that the Christ in the blind man could not refuse to come forth. But do not let this put you off from trying. The effect will be immediate in that you will know that you are resonating with the highest in you, that you are consciously taking steps towards becoming a Christ.

Dear Ones, I want to say to you, open your eyes and see! Open your spiritual eye to see only beauty around you and in all your fellow humans.

Open your mouth and speak only beauty.

Open your ears and hear only beauty.

6

FROM DIRECTION
TO DIMENSION

THE POINT at which your soul guides your life to make the first conscious steps on the path of growth is when you begin to exchange direction for dimension. As the desire to add dimension to your life increases so your interest in following the path of direction, of succeeding only in earthly terms, begins to diminish. The need to realise personal ambitions and maintain status in the eyes of others is no longer a driving force in your life. It is replaced by a desire to simplify your life and a longing for freedom. How often we hear your cries of 'I want to be free!' emerging from the prisons you have made for yourselves.

For some though the idea of direction, ambition, status, has never occurred; they have not been born to follow such a clearly definable path and may be harshly judged by their society, even referred to as drifters. They are not luckier because they have nothing to lose, for their pain has been in their wilderness years, without conscious direction and facing the disapproval of parents and society because their lives are not conforming to linear convention. But do you make a rose wrong because it flowers later than the daffodil?

Because of their inherent sensitivity those who are naturally dimensional will much more easily absorb the projections of others and act them out. Because their sense of self will develop later they will become easy prey for those whose common sense arguments readily undermine their emerging selves. Their self healing work is therefore to separate themselves out from the insecurities imposed upon them by those who either do not understand them or are unconsciously jealous of their evolved state. This is essential for their self acceptance and empowerment, and by owning who they truly are the groundwork for their larger purpose is then laid. They also have a major task in transforming their greatest gift, their sensitivity, into something that works for them and not against them. Instead of being like a thin skin which makes them vulnerable, it needs to be like a shining armour which not only deflects that which is harmful but which easily reflects light. In such beings sensitivity is a mark of their potential warriorhood, and that there is a role for them in the Vanguard Army, the front line of those whose task it is to bring transformation and healing upon your planet.

Those who are inherently dimensional are not however victims of a directional world. Their souls have made a deliberate decision to be born into a seemingly alien and hostile environment so that their first task may be to access the strength and courage to be true to themselves, even in the face of the cruelest ridicule and judgement. More and more you will find this the case in your society and such people deserve your applause as much as those who excel in a chosen direction. I want to say especially to parents now, that if your child does not seem to have found what he or she wants to do in life it is most probably because their soul is waiting for a special calling that happens in Divine time, not according to the generally accepted stages of human development or your wishes for them. Countless souls are incarnating at this time who have encoded within them a plan relevant to this all important time in mankind's and your planet's evolution but outside society's expectations. All the time that they are waiting to birth their vocation they are journeying in a different way, mining their inner resources through experience, and establishing a sense of self that is based upon being rather than doing. If such a soul chooses to come into your family, celebrate that fact. Let them be your teachers even! Let your observations of them help to mould you into a more dimensional being. And as parents, make the gift you bring above all others to your children the certainty that they are truly seen and acknowledged in their souls by you.

For so many of you, my dear friends on Earth, still suffer from the fact that you were not recognised for the special soul that you are in the first hours and days of your life. Had you had the gift of speech then you might have said to your parents 'Hey, Mum, Dad, can't you see, its me! ME!' But of course all they could perceive was the baby whom they loved as best they could. The knock-on effect of not being recognised was to leave you with the assumption that there was something wrong with you and that if you were to receive even a modicum of your needs you must turn your attention to pleasing them first. So began the habit of giving your power away. So too began the struggle to understand the meaning of self love. But also so were the seeds of your life of compassion and service to others first sown.

When the caterpillar decides it is time to create a cocoon this is when it decides to exchange direction for dimension. No more a life of crawling around on a leaf satisfying its appetite, it lets go of its life so far, even to the point of giving up its whole identity and entering into nothingness before becoming that winged beauty. Remember, a caterpillar does not become a butterfly; a caterpillar becomes a squidgy mess and the squidgy mess becomes a butterfly.

Your transition from a directional to dimensional being will be as total but the time it takes and the intensity of the experience is not fixed. That depends on the resistance to change and the attachments to the old life and the old self. The greater the investment in the material life and belief in the persona, the darker the night of the soul that will follow for there will be more to lose, except that of course in this instance the notion of giving up is illusory for what will take its place is of infinitely greater value. Without a doubt, there can be no halfway fullness; you cannot have your cake and eat it. Some may be tempted, especially those whose persona has worked well for them, but spirituality cannot ever be the frame to enhance your persona, for then it will be as inauthentic as the gilt that coats the frame; instead the dimensional journey is the peeling away of the overlays and reworkings that conceal the Old Master which when restored does not need a frame to increase its value.

Whatever, none will be immune from having to say 'I don't know who I am any more'. Nor can anyone avoid the changes that need to take place in every cell of your body which might result in unfamiliar symptoms which the professionals will be unable to diagnose. They will probably tell you that it is all psychosomatic. You might find too that qualities you once cherished like orderliness or attention to detail will change. You may feel as if you are losing your memory. You may want to spend more time on your own than you are used to. You may feel detached from your friends and lonely for someone who can really understand you and see into the new depths that are opening up in you. You may be more volatile in your moods and find yourself crying more than before and feeling very angry, all the emotions that you have had to bury for so long in order to win love and approval.

Such change occurs outside time, and outside all parameters of human mind control. The decision to transform is not a conscious one, just as a flower does not have to make a conscious decision to open. I say this, Dear Ones, only to remind you that will-power alone is insufficient to bring about the changes I am talking about, for then there can be little room for humility. You might want to use will-power or mind-power if you see spiritual growth as being a way to become a nicer person or to feel better about yourself or even to impress others. Such goals will be a hindrance to your journey for they are born out of your insecurity and not your soul's desire. The truly dimensional person does not need to talk about their spirituality or gifts for they are as normal to them as breathing. The one who still has one foot in the path of direction will want to find a way to add it to his curriculum vitae along with his other qualifications.

Just as when the tree matures and grows taller more branches emerge, so as you mature spiritually more dimensions are born in you. But although the symptoms of change can be recognised and felt, the resulting new dimensions are not so easy to define for they are beyond ego. You will find, however, that just as the lower branches of the tree reap a poorer harvest than the young ones nearer to the sun, so too will human talents and even so-called gifts of the spirit, psychic gifts, which so many of you deem so important now as a measure of spiritual attainment, not bring you any nourishment any more.

None of these will satisfy you or serve you any longer. Neither your intellectual abilities or powers of reason; neither your ability to channel or predict the future; neither your ability to charm and attract others to you or validation by any feedback from another person;

neither having the resources to buy whatever you want or by any outer display of material accomplishment. You will become numb to the stimulus these once provided. It may even feel as if nothing is working in your life any more.

As for the freedom you crave it is in fact a symptom of a soul's hunger to live in an indefinable space, to empty yourself so that unburdened you may rise up to be filled with life anew, or simply to rest. How tired we see many of you and this is because you are having to live a life of such compromise because you have become so bound up with the responsibilities and survival issues that living in a three dimensional world brings with it. But accompanying these feelings is also so much fear; fear of what others may think, fear of how you could possibly survive financially. Oh that you could see over the fence to see how perfectly all will turn out you would not resist for any reason the slide into living dimensionally.

Whatever your worst fears are, Dear Ones, imagine them as having come true, imagine living with them, and you will find that life is not as bad as you thought it would be, that you still live and love and are loved, and having confronted those fears they will no longer run your life as before.

Free of fear and attachment to any false persona your life can unfold magically and mystically. With such mysticism will come mystery also, for God moves in mysterious ways to reveal Her love for you. Then you will need to train yourself to release the need to understand for understanding, a process of the mind, becomes a limitation to discovering deeper mysteries which are revealed in the expanding of the heart.

Let life become your own magical mystery tour! The dimensional being does not need the security of knowing by any means other than his faith that all is well always and such faith will be continually rewarded by demonstration of Grace working in his life.

If this is your journey now, celebrate it and surrender to it. We watch over you as you go through these and all other changes that are inextricably a part of the journey plotted by your soul. Our most loving act is not to smooth out the more painful parts, even though we hear all too clearly your cries for help, but to simply allow you to go through this essential preparation. As often as we can we seek to remind you that you are not alone, that there is a purpose to everything. If you look hard enough you will notice our 'visiting cards' for it is not our way to conceal ourselves from you. We can use so many ways to reach you that if you could see them all you would marvel at our inventiveness and certainly your sense of humour would be restored to you had you lost it. My own special 'visiting card' is a white feather and some of my friends have found these turning up at times of need in places where you would least expect to find one. You do not need to ask for my help before I will bring you one; indeed I would rather you did not ask me for help at all but that in faith you went straight to the Highest, the One whom we all serve.

7

CHANGING
CIRCUMSTANCES

DO NOT be trapped into thinking that as you enter upon the path of growth that every circumstance in your life must change.

It works like this. You are in a very tall building, in one of the lower floors. You are tired of the ground plan at that level so you enter into the elevator and for a while you are in a space that allows no sense of relation to ground or sky, only a vague sense of movement. Then the doors open and you walk out to find that everything is exactly the same as the floor you had just left, that is until you go to the window. Then you see that you have a much higher view!

At this new level you are not drawn to look downwards at the frenetic activity you could once see in such detail and consider your relationship to it. On this new level you can be more detached from all of that and instead allow your vision to be drawn towards broader landscapes and new horizons.

So, Dear Ones, it is not in changing the circumstances of your life the immediate solution is provided but it is in changing your relationship to those circumstances so that you can have a higher view of them and be less attached at an ego level to the nature of your role there.

So often I hear from my friends the beautiful news of their desire to help people, perhaps by practising some healing technique or other. At the same time they feel unhappy with their working lives and feel if only they could give up their work and be full-time healers instead they must be nearer to fulfilling their life purpose.

But this cannot be the case yet, for it is in the workplace that there are those who could most benefit from having a healer amongst them who by their very presence could raise the energy of the working environment and so offer them the opportunity for a higher view. It may not be work to satisfy the ego, for signs of appreciation may be few and far between, but that has never been a motive to heal.

If you are one of those who are looking for an escape from your current working life then your heart will probably sink when you read these words. But I am not inferring that you face instead a life sentence of working within such an energy. Remember I only say that to make such changes is not the immediate solution, for if everyone in every walk of life saw a journey of transformation as being one that offered an instant escape route from a working life that was not obviously one of service then the transformation in every walk of life could never happen.

Consider also that you may be one of our moles, an as yet secret agent of the Light awaiting your orders to begin your work. There is not one area of human activity that does not contain a 'mole'; not one major organisation, or political party, or industry, or company, or workplace or any place of influence exists where one of God's servants is not patiently biding his or her time, waiting for 'their hour to come' when their true identity can be revealed. Few will be conscious of the role that awaits them and the larger implications surrounding their emergence. Like many of you it may just be an indefinable feeling of having a task to perform in this life, of knowing that you are on Earth for a specific reason.

In your history books you will find obvious examples of such men and women on whose shoulders destiny placed the burden of altering the course of history for good. The beloved Mahatma, the politician Churchill, the leader Mandela and many more less celebrated than these. Each came to the role for which you know them after years in the wilderness, followed by the trumpet call of destiny.

The laws affecting the unfolding of the destiny of these souls are the same for you. You cannot dictate the timing of your emergence anymore than the flower seed hidden amongst the infinite grains of desert sand can decide upon its flowering. It must wait for the gentle rain to fall from heaven; then it and all the countless other invisible seeds can instantly transform what was once barren into a blaze of colour and lushness.

It is easy to view despairingly your business and political worlds and see them as spiritually barren as the desert is of vegetation. But now you know that it is not really so, for you are there, and countless others like you, at every level of power and authority, encoded with the mission to bring freedom through Truth to every walk of life. We ask you only to wait in faith and trust for the right moment for the heavens to open and for the light of the Christ to pour down upon you the grace to transform your area of desert into a place of beauty.

8

EBB
AND FLOW

IT IS only human that you strive to maintain a sense of well-being on every level. And as you follow your spiritual journey even more you hope, and perhaps expect to live in a state of well-being that if you were a pussy cat would have you purring incessantly.

But the well-being that many of you believe is reflecting having arrived somewhere special is usually a fairly superficial sensation that inevitably passes and then you feel disappointed or as if you have failed because once again you find yourself dealing with the harsher realities of life. That feeling of inner peace and self empowerment is replaced by the all too familiar feelings of disconnection and longing. Your prayers of gratitude become once again cries for help and guidance.

The solution, Dear Ones, is not to put too much importance on such feelings that, like the tides of the ocean, ebb and flow beyond your control. And like the ocean, the surface has many moods, from utter calm to raging storms, but you only have to go a little way below the surface to find a place of peace and calm that is constant. So it is your task to go behind all the changing sensations and find that place of stillness that is your connectedness to Source. Your faith in your source needs be based on that experience of constancy not on those brief periods of bliss that may arise as a result of your spiritual practices. If you base your faith in God and the unseen world on such experiences, there will always remain doubt.

There are of course those special moments of connectedness which come out of the blue. They cannot be manufactured by any spiritual practice. Those feelings of being swept up into a vortex of energy when time stands still and you feel as if you have been pumped up like a balloon, come to you through Grace and what is pumped into you is Love. At such times you will certainly undergo a permanent vibrational lift that is preparing you for something. I deliberately do not specify what, as I do not want you then to be attached to any outcome as I do not want you to be attached to the sensation itself and wish for it to last forever. Just be grateful that you have had it and let it go.

But let us not dismiss entirely the ebb and flow of conscious states. When the tide is out it is your chance for a bit of spiritual and psychological beach-combing. What flotsam and jetsam of unresolved pain has been exposed by the outgoing tide? Or what treasures of deeper insight have been uncovered? Use this time well, for surely the tide will come in again and these rich pickings will be lost in the euphoria of such fullness again experienced.

Meanwhile out on the ocean, the sailor knows that he cannot be becalmed forever, for he needs a wind to take him nearer to his destination. And when the storm rages he will be reminded of that little boat that was once tossed about on the Sea of Galilee with Jesus sleeping peacefully in its bow.

9

CELEBRATION!

CELEBRATION! is my favourite word.

Every day find something to celebrate. It does not matter how small. If you cannot find anything in your own life to celebrate maybe you will find something in a loved one's life to celebrate. And you will find that the more you celebrate the more you will find to celebrate, until life becomes a celebration.

Celebrate by lighting a candle with a prayer of gratitude and praise on your lips.

Celebrate by treating yourself.

Celebrate by giving someone else a treat.

Celebrate by going within to meet the source of all joy that lives in your own heart.

And there is no better way to guarantee my presence with you than to celebrate. I never miss a party!

10

GANG MEMBERS SOUGHT

I HAVE one rule for anyone who may be interested in joining my gang and that is NEVER MAKE YOURSELF WRONG!

You do not make a rosebud wrong because it is not yet in full bloom. You know that as the warmth of the sun continues to shine upon it it will open.

You do not make you finger wrong if when you cut it it bleeds. Instead you clean that wound and you bind it, and protect it and then you take the binding off and expose it to the light and the air for the healing to be complete. You love it!

So why make yourself wrong because your potential to live as a Christed Being is not yet fully realised or because you sometimes act out of your woundedness.

We know full well that those of you whose inner vision is set upon Oneness with God are consciously inviting the light to shine upon you to raise you up and are working hard on the healing of your wounds.

We do not judge you or say amongst ourselves 'tut tut, the naughty child', when sometimes you act in a way that does not resonate with the highest in you, nor must you judge yourself but instead be infinitely forgiving and compassionate towards yourself as you aspire to be towards others.

And remember, when 'you' *DO* achieve that Oneness we are not going to love you any more than we do now because we *CANNOT* love you more than we do now!

Dear Ones, accept yourselves as being perfect for you now, with all that you would like to change. Accept your lives as being perfect for now. Accepting perfection as the truth of you now and your life now is taking the path of non resistance. If you make yourselves wrong or your life wrong there is automatically a contraction taking place in your heart and so creating a resistance to the flow of Love, the flow of life.

Just by saying to yourself as an affirmation 'I am perfect now' will raise your vibration above the level of where you are now because IT IS TRUE! Making yourself wrong, affirming your imperfection and 'sinfulness', serves only to entrap you in a pattern of ups and downs in your life because you will always keep the redemptive power of Unconditional Divine Love out of your life. 'And I will raise all men up unto me!' The 'I', the Christ, the Perfect in you, will raise you up to the Oneness.

So please, come and join my gang!

11

PATIENCE

I WONDER how many times you have been told in your life to be patient.

When I tell you to be patient I do not mean that you must go into a corner and twiddle your thumbs, waiting for something to happen.

To be patient is to be in the now, knowing that now everything is perfect as it is.

To be patient is to do whatever task is before you with consciousness and love, even if it is peeling the potatoes or clearing up the mess your kids have made.

Impatience is the opposite of compatience, or compassion. When you are impatient with someone you are not being compassionate towards them.

Think of all the times you have been enjoying yourself and have then remarked 'Doesn't time fly when you are enjoying yourself!' That is because when you are enjoying yourself you are so absorbed in what you are doing that the past and the future no longer exist. There is only the now.

So not only does time go faster when you are in the now, thus making what you are impatient about come to you much more quickly, but to be in the now is to be in a state of joy.

Until you can master this be patient with yourself!

12

MEDITATION

DEAR ONES, I see so many of you struggling in your attempts to meditate. Perhaps it is because you are expecting too much from yourself or are worried that you are using the wrong method. Perhaps you compare your experience with that of others and therefore come to the conclusion that you are doing it wrong or are no good at it. Perhaps your soul has bad memories of it from past lives or that you have done so much of it in your soul's history that it is just inappropriate for your life now. Whatever, you do not have to feel bad or guilty or handicapped because now you cannot do it.

Your goal is not to be able to meditate for two hours a day as some say you should but to aim to make all your life a meditation. That is to be able to live through any experience that daily life throws at you and not to lose your contact with that place of stillness. Similarly if you believe that praying is something you do for a few minutes each evening by your bed, how can you make your life a prayer.

To be unable to meditate is not such a serious thing you know. Many great souls have advanced far on their journey without this practice. Instead they have enjoyed other activities such as contemplation or performing Japa or reciting a mantra, or just loving their neighbour.

If you have found it difficult to empty your mind of thoughts which is meditation, you may find it easier to fill your mind with thoughts, but not just any old thoughts! Contemplation is an experience of going within, as meditation is, but with a thought. It is like day dreaming which I am sure many of you are very good at, but with a bit more focus. You do not have to close your eyes or sit in an uncomfortable position to do it. You can even be doing something else at the same time, but something that requires only minimal concentration.

You may choose to contemplate or reflect upon, which is the same thing, something you have just read in one of your spiritual books and as you begin to think about something that has struck a chord your mind wanders, not aimlessly, but along a connected train of thought. These thoughts come as you engage your Higher Self or maybe even your guides, who take advantage of your openness then to bring you to a deeper understanding or greater appreciation of the text. As this happens you may feel your heart expanding and energy coming into your body as this new insight percolates deeper into your consciousness.

You may prefer to contemplate the beauty of a sunset or a leaf or the little insect that crawls across your hand, all reflecting back to you the truth of perfection everywhere. My choice for you as a subject to contemplate would be your own oneness with God and therefore your perfection.

And if that sounds difficult, try performing Japa as our Hindu friends do. For this all you need to do is to take the name of your favourite embodiment of the Divine and say that name over and over again. You may want to choose Jesus, or Mohammed, or the Holy Mother or your favourite saint. As you say their name over and over again you will draw their energy to you and, just as with contemplation, after a time you will feel a glow in your heart. Think of the times when you have been in love and how you felt when you thought of your beloved. Doing Japa can open your heart in the same way to love one of these great Masters and they can love you back.

And if all of this fails, it does not matter. There is no judgement. We know you. God sees deeper into your heart than any human and finds treasures already there beyond your wildest imagination. Just do the best you can. Remember, you are perfect as you are.

13

HAVING A
LOVE FEAST

DEAR FRIENDS who are following the path of self-healing and of service to the world, you need each other!

I cannot emphasise enough the need for you to have fellowship amongst those who share your deepest and highest intentions. Too many of you hide away for fear of losing energy to others or because you seek affection in those with whom you wish to socialise.

Come together often, like the first disciples did, to break the bread and drink the wine. Meet together in an upper room where you are one with your higher mind and heart, to prepare a Love Feast together with your friends.

Let your shared discipleship be the point of contact so that you speak one language together, the language of the heart; do not be drawn into the cellar of your mind by gossip and idle talk of those who are not present.

Let your shared discipleship reveal itself in laughter and fun as much as in the serious work of sending out the Light for a joyful countenance needs to be the mark of one who knows Truth.

Let the spirit of your gathering be one of celebration. Let all within it spring from that one energy; celebration of each others company, celebration of the food you are eating, celebration of your accomplishments since you last met, celebration of the beauty of a bird song you heard that day, of the first rose to bloom in your garden, of a healed relationship. The possibilities are endless.

With so much celebration you may rise from your upper room to the penthouse of your consciousness. With so much celebration your heart is going to be bursting with thankfulness and praise. Consciously link together in that spirit, for what better spirit could one be in to send the Light, than one of thankfulness and praise. Consciously link yourselves to all such groups meeting around the world in the same spirit. Do not forget that your shared discipleship includes those guides and angels who work with you from the world of Light. Welcome them into your midst and know that those of you present in a physical body will be heavily out numbered by those who are not.

In the part of your gathering when you are sending out the light to heal others, do not put limits on how far that Light can go, for time and space are not the issue here, but do not forget your immediate vicinity either and the community in which you live because your presence can do much to bring healing and good neighbourliness there. Love your neighbours! Do not put limits on your belief as to what the Light can accomplish; be willing to risk a miracle happening as a result of your sacred intention. It can only give you another reason to celebrate!

As you peak out the names of those who you know who you are sending their healing to, see them as already healed, as radiantly happy, as filled with the Light of Divine Love. You can send Light to Nations too, to areas of conflict and human suffering and not forgetting your dear planet Earth. See in your mind's eye all as healed *NOW*, as perfect *NOW*! Do not diminish the power of the Light to work by any judgment of the situations you hope for it to transform or by thinking that what you do is only a drop in the ocean. The ocean is made up of drops.

I suggest that you write the names of all of those to whom you are sending the Light of healing in a book and that every day a candle is lit by that book with a dedication. You can take it in turns to have the book in your home.

And Dear Ones, when your Belovéd Master Jesus told you that when two or more are gathered in His name that He will be there also, He meant it! Now, go and enjoy yourselves.

14

AFFIRMATION

I SEE many of you becoming disappointed because your affirmations do not work, especially when you use them to draw something to you.

The reason for this is often because your affirmations do not contain Truth and so your efforts are hampered by powerful unconscious beliefs.

If for example you affirm 'All the money I need is now coming to me' a little voice inside you, a saboteur, is going to say back to you 'Oh yeah? Prove it!' But if you were to affirm instead simply 'I am one with abundance, so all my needs are now met' your saboteur can do nothing because It's a Truth, and what you want can more easily come to you.

Truth as I mean it here are the Divine Laws such as the law of attraction, the law of abundance, the law of compensation (a lot of people forget that one), the law of cause and effect. They usually work hand in hand.

The law of attraction is clear in its meaning. Like attracts like but also unlike repels unlike. Do not forget that part of it. So if you are affirming for a partner my advice to you is to draw up a shopping list of all the qualities you are looking for and if you can find anything on that list that you do not yet possess yourself then make it yours. Your affirmation must then begin with the words 'I am one with the law of attraction...'

This law can be explained in this way too. You have a saying 'Money makes money' because it seems as if rich people have no problems attracting more money to them. The way this works is not that they are better at investments than a poorer person but that their consciousness of abundance can attract further abundance, in the form that they already have it. They may be able to attract a lot of financial abundance but be lonely and living a loveless existence. Someone with a lot of love within them will attract a lot of love to them.

The law of abundance states that there is no lack of anything anywhere in the Universe. You may be overdrawn at your High Street Bank but in the Cosmic Bank you have limitless credit... and no charges. You can withdraw as much as you want from it if you can just believe that,regardless of how it looks in your situation, a way always exists for your needs to be met if you allow it.

But remember, Dear Ones, abundance is a state of being, not a state of having. There are those who have everything but feel poor and those who have nothing but feel rich. Before you affirm for what you want from this law be clear within yourself that what you are asking for is really what you need and not to prop up a feeling of inner impoverishment.

The law of compensation states that if for whatever reason you are called upon to let something or someone go from your life you will always be compensated for by something of greater value, if that is truly your belief. If not you may find yourself spiralling down into an attitude of self-pity or victim consciousness.

Many of you are being called upon to give up much at the moment which is why we want to remind you of that law. It may be that the replacement will not come immediately, for to be open to something greater you have to grow a bit. And perhaps what will come back to you will be in a different form from what you have had to let go of but it will always be to enrich your inner life. If you were to lose money the compensation may be in a new understanding about true abundance so you can have a healthy relationship with money; if you were to lose a relationship the compensation may be in the guidance you will receive to point out the roots of an old pattern of losing relationships so that the law of attraction can work for you to bring you your heart's desire.

Be willing to let go all the time for it is the nature of your soul's journey. Growing in this way is not about addition, it is about subtraction, reducing all down to its purest essence. But I must add that we ask you to sacrifice nothing, except perhaps sacrifice itself.

There are no spiritual brownie points in sacrifice as a pious intent, but by your faith in the law of compensation you will grow immeasurably and you will witness miracle after miracle. The affirmation for this law is only when you see something leaving your life to acknowledge in your heart and mind that you are one with it and to follow the path of non-resistance.

But Dear Ones, it has to be said that if you need to affirm for anything that you currently lack, not only physical and material things but even a state of awareness you are showing that you still need to heal the fundamental belief in separation from God, your source. Begin with that and all else will be added unto you without ever having to practice affirmations. Then lack will not be lack, aloneness will not be aloneness. You will find grace filling every corner of your life. You will have faith to surrender all to God; you will only know gratitude and you will want to express in the prayer that you will then find so easy to say 'Thy will be done!'

15

PAST LIVES

I AM often asked why you do not incarnate with the memory of your past lives? There are two main reasons for this.

Firstly, for the same reason that you would not go into an examination with the answers written on the back of your hand; it would be cheating. If you could remember your past life you would know in advance what specific lessons you still had to learn in this life, so where would be the learning and where would be the need for faith?

The second reason is that most of you have a hard enough time living in the now with just this life's painful experiences to integrate. How would you cope if you had the memory of fifty or a hundred lives to integrate? I think some of the more squeamish amongst you might have an especially hard time for an essential part of evolution has been to experience just about everything that life can throw at you. If you could remember the life when you were a powerful and rich ruler you might bask happily in that memory. But if you could remember the times that you were burnt at the stake or boiled in oil then you have the recipe for a lot of nightmares. Do I make my point? And you know, Dear Ones, you must credit your soul with possessing some degree of wisdom for guiding you to a life now that contains all the raw materials you need *NOW* for your evolution.

I do not want to sound like a killjoy but I do not recommend regressions into past lives as a way of healing problems of this life. I know how you like to dine out on your escapades a few centuries ago or to find an explanation for your present suffering in the dim and distant past. I know also that many of you believe you have been helped by discovering facts about your past lives.

But remember, for most of you who believe in reincarnation this is a new belief; it is not one that you were born with and it is only now that you have broken out of the imposed belief systems of your early life that you accept reincarnation as a reality. You should also know that the belief in reincarnation is shared by countless millions of people on Earth, more than those who do not believe in it. But for the majority of such believers living with such a belief does not arouse any curiosity about what their past lives may have been; with an inherent belief in Divine justice it provides a path to acceptance of the conditions of their present lives and therefore a way to live more peacefully in the now, without knowing the details.

You would be able to share the same philosophy were not the notion of victim hood so much a part of your inherited belief systems. A truly devout Buddhist does not see himself as an innocent victim nor would he be interested to know what karma had drawn him to his present situation. He would just accept and work hard to live better. So to be regressed into a past life so that you know why something is going wrong in this life is to judge your life in terms of right or wrong, good or bad, or in other words to be dis-empowered by the nature of duality. It is also to overlook the fact that the wisdom of your soul has made sure to choose conditions for this life that provide all the raw materials you need for your growing now. It would be a cruel imposition by a soul to create circumstances of blockage that could only be removed by undergoing regression. If such a blockage can be seen for what it really is, a thought form which cannot be bound by time and which in truth has about as much substance as the wispiest cloud in a summer sky, then it is possible to see how everything can be healed by being fully present in the now.

I would also say that there is no fool-proof method available to you for remembering or entering past lives that excludes any risk of unconscious interference by the person being regressed. When curiosity is a motive then that too provides fertile ground for the imagination to run riot and what may then be experienced as a past life will be a pictorial representation of an unconscious state relating to the now.

You would be far better to trust your gut feelings about where or when you might have lived in the past. Trust those feelings of attraction or repulsion to certain places. Trust too the feelings of kinship with people in your life, even when the attraction may wane or they may eventually hurt you for nobody is going to come into your life to play a significant role who is not an old friend. Enjoy this life especially as one that has seen and will continue to see many reunions with fellow travellers from down the ages, members of your soul tribe to whom you can be immensely grateful for the part they have played in your reaching your present level of evolution.

That sounds like a good enough reason for celebration to me!

16

KARMA

OF ALL the words that have entered into your vocabulary since moving towards your New Age beliefs, surely the most abused and misunderstood is 'Karma'.

Having quite rightly rejected the orthodox Christian teaching that wishes to control you by labelling you as a sinner, many of you have chosen karma instead as an excuse for not owning your inherent Christhood. Not only that but your readiness to believe in others karma provides a perfect excuse not to make the effort to respond to their pain with compassion. 'That's their karma' you may say to yourself when hearing of someone's difficulties. Can you not see that by the same token such an uncompassionate response can only create negative karma for you, whereas a compassionate response might erase any karma you may have.

Dear Ones, I have to warn you against such superficial assumptions that every event in a person's life arises out of their karma. When I observe the suffering of my friends on Earth, in a very few cases only, is karma the cause. More often than not suffering is there as a symptom of the soul's intent to live compassionately and play a humble role in bringing love and healing to your world.

Those of you with an orthodox Christian background will be all too familiar with the teaching 'Judge not that you be not judged'. Others may well be familiar also with the wisdom of the Native American who would say instead 'May I judge no man until I have walked for two moons in his moccasins'. I should like to elaborate on that in this context of karma.

If you were to have the privilege to walk in another man's moccasins, in other words to enter into his being, you would discover an awful lot about him. You would become aware of the circumstances that had shaped his life. You would feel his fears; you would know his deepest and highest desires; you would feel his guilt and shame; you would experience how much, or how little, love there was in his life; you would know about the suffering he had endured quietly for which the rest of the world would never give him credit and the courage with which he faced his adversity; you might know all the little loving acts of loving kindness performed, again without anybody else knowing; you might even know something about his past lives; and if he knew you, you could see yourself through another's eyes which might be very shocking and humbling. Think on, Dear Ones, try to imagine doing this with those who you feel antagonistic towards or whose suffering you might earlier have dismissed as being simply their karma. Do this until you feel your heart beginning to expand with love and praise, having now received a glimmer of understanding of this perfect law.

What I am sure of is that in most cases you would be very happy to return to your own shoes after those two moons, and be feeling much more compassionate towards yourself as a result. I would pray also that you would return to your shoes with one more essential quality, humility, which along with compassion and kindness must form the bedrock of your spirituality.

And if you were to find that you were reluctant to return to your own shoes, then pray for the courage to endure and learn the lessons which the circumstances of your life have brought you. Remember, everything in life is for you. Nothing is against you.

Of course Karma, the law of sowing and reaping, is an unavoidable fact of life but many of you who have timed your visit to Earth to play your part in the changes, arrive with a clean sheet or at least with your karma on a back burner. Your presence in your body now is because you have chosen to come and serve only. You can never imagine how sweet those words sound to me 'I want to help other people'.

If the opportunities to serve have not yet arrived, then it could be that you are one of those whose lives can be divided into two parts; the first part being where you tie up all the loose ends of the past, including your karma, and the second where your larger purpose is enacted. But those who have a clean sheet may find their lives similarly divided, where the first part is difficult and the second where life opens up. Then the suffering is to break open the heart that the sweet essence of compassion be released.

But the fact is in your human form, you will never know which is which. Nor should it be of any interest to you to know. Instead concentrate upon the quiet sowing of seeds of love, kindness and compassion; then the nature of the harvest, the same being returned to you, is guaranteed.

17

FAST FORWARD

IT IS no longer the older amongst you who can get away with saying that the years are going by more quickly because it is now a truth that affects everyone. The years are going by faster but rest assured, Dear Ones, it does not mean that your lives will be shorter.

Those of you who are attracted to the apocalyptic scenario may also view the events of your world as a sign that things are hotting up. And you would be.right too in a manner of speaking for what happens when you heat something? The atoms move faster.

And of course we must not forget those countless pious souls down through the centuries who embraced prolonged periods of abstinence from food as a part of their spiritual practices. They fasted! As a result of their practices the vibrations of their body went faster.

From around two thousand years ago up until this period of history when your New Age consciousness began to enter in, the energy of Light shining on your planet has been fairly constant. There has been the odd fluctuation and it is for good reason that your history books refer to the Dark Ages and the Renaissance Period. During this time every soul has of course had the opportunity to evolve within the framework of the traditions and religions of where they incarnated. But now as you are well aware God has His hand on the dimmer switch and is turning the power up and none can be immune from its effect.

For you dear friends whom I address, it means that you may now be living at a level of understanding that you have never known in all your lives before. You therefore find yourselves now in terms of consciousness in a place without a map with only the heavenly bodies, your guides and angels, your higher self, to guide you. With their help you are being forced to learn new ways to operate within life, for the old ways, the laws of man, no longer serve you or satisfy your needs.

And with the quickening vibrations and the subsequent distortion to linear time, it means that for the first time in all your history of earthly life you can embrace in your present embodiment two incarnations worth of experience. In other words the experiences that at an earlier time in history might have required at least two incarnations to undergo, you are doing in one. In that sense two into one definitely does go!

But there is another angle to this which is the heart of this message for I am sure that if this embodiment is to contain two incarnations you want the second one to be better than the first! At the very least it can be as distinct from the one you are now in as it is from your last embodiment. At the very most it can be as a fully realised human being, living in heaven on earth.

The key, is quite simply in letting go of the past, for to fail to do so means that the weight of the past goes forward with you into your new 'incarnation'. And the past, with all the associated feelings, is in your body.

It is not surprising that so many of you find it hard to always be fully in your body and are therefore so ungrounded. Unless you are a trained dancer it is not easy to maintain poise while doing the splits but I see many of you doing just that, pulling in two directions. And you wonder why your life does not seem to be progressing as smoothly as you would like!

The practice of fasting can of course have an effect if combined with other spiritual practices but as most contemporary lifestyles do not allow you to take sufficient time out it will accomplish little for you. As a token of intent, to fast for one or two days a month is better than nothing and has the added advantage of giving some of your bodily functions a rest and an opportunity for a bit of detoxification.

I want to suggest ways that are much easier than that Dear Ones. You have most probably spent enough long periods of fasting in your earthly lives to last you for a long time, unless you receive a clear calling to do so.

You can let go of the past in a spirit of acceptance that all that has been in your life has been as it could only be and therefore everyone who has been in your life has been there because they needed to be. What place is there then for any resentment or anger. Does forgiveness not become easier then? Does it then not become easier to live in a spirit of thankfulness and praise... and celebration!

If you are seeking a new spiritual practice that is relevant to your evolution now then I suggest you focus every day upon the harmonisation of every cell of your body with the new energies as they reach your earth plane. They are increasing in frequency every day so tune up to them every day. Develop a sense of your whole beingness, your physical as well as your subtle bodies, as a vibration and think of it resonating perfectly with the highest frequency it can carry. You could even do this before you go to sleep and ask for the process to take place during the night. In turn your body may give you messages as to any other supportive measures you could take to help it in the task you have given it.

And how about giving yourself some practice at living without your clocks and watches! Give yourself days when you are not ruled by linear time and not only will you be amazed at how much you get done but you will also discover your body's true rhythm. It is also important for the future for as the quickening on earth builds up any mechanism that reflects linear time or operates under it will break down. And I do not want you to waste time trying to work out the implications of this for your world now; when you need to understand it you will, and not before! As Brother Paul wrote in his hymn to Love '...at present I am learning bit by bit but then I shall understand, as I have always been understood.'

Just know that when the moment comes that you have raised your vibration sufficiently to detach from linear time you will not find yourself becoming unpunctual or missing important meetings because there will be many others vibrating in harmony with you and you will be able to communicate by quite other means. You will be masters of telepathy. And just as you may now occasionally get a hunch that you should go to a certain place at a certain time, so this will become normal for you. When you have broken away from your present three dimensional reality the law of synchronicity can operate much more freely. Your every step will be perfectly timed for you will all be dancing to the same tune.

There may be some casualties as a result of this change, astrologers for example, whose science is based upon fixed time. It will not be possible to predict the stages in someone's life or even the influences that the planets assert within linear time, because you will have to move to a place beyond any such external influence.

And those of course who wish to remain in control of the pace of their lives will have a fall. Imagine you are walking forward on an ever accelerating moving walkway and trying to progress at the same pace as you would walk normally. There will come a point when you can only do this by walking backwards until you lose your balance and fall off. There will be many such casualties but they are not loved any the less for it and will be well cared for.

And Dear Ones, the fact that linear time is speeding up will certainly not mean that your life will be shorter, unless of course you choose to remain living with an investment in linear time. Yes, physical laws state that dense matter which your bodies may now consist of has a limited life span but as you work at keeping up with the increasing vibrations and as you deepen your contact with the Source through your devotional practices that dense matter becomes more light filled and is not subject to the same laws of decay anymore! This has been proved in cases within your lifetime even where the physical bodies of illumined souls have remained intact long after the spirit's departure.

One disadvantage of this for some is that Birthdays will become meaningless but you will have countless other reasons to celebrate instead. Nor will you be interested in measuring lifetimes by their length or even be concerned about the end for when you have ascended to that level of consciousness when time is irrelevant it will be because you will have penetrated the veil that now separates our two worlds.

It is then that you will fully understand the illusion that is death and that you cannot die for the life of you!

18

THE
GREENHOUSE EFFECT

THOSE WHO coined the expression the greenhouse effect to describe the effect of various gas emissions upon your planet's atmosphere could never have been aware of how this definition also perfectly describes the effect upon the human soul of the spiritual forces now working in the ethers.

If I could take as an example just one practical use of a greenhouse, a space where the forces of the sun through glass hastens the growth of a plant, you can understand how, counter to the negative impact of the release of gases into the Earth's atmosphere, the rays of the cosmic sun are encouraging in friends like you an acceleration in your spiritual growth so that you may release into the world the beauty of your spiritual energy, an energy far more intoxicating than those so-called greenhouse gases are toxic.

We know, Dear Ones, that this time of accelerated growth is uncomfortable at times. You experience your growing pains in the same way as you did when you were an adolescent. In fact you might feel far from loving while it takes place and ask yourselves questions like 'What's it all for? Who wants to be spiritual anyway if this is what it is going to feel like?' You may look enviously at those who lead such simple lives, as you perceive them, and wish that yours could be that simple again. But you also know that the complexities that are a part of being you make that impossible. You must accept it, that life as you once knew it has had its day, and I do not mean just your own personal life. Life, human existence, especially for conscious beings like yourself now but eventually for everyone, will never be quite the same again.

This will not be because of what are judged as the negative things happening on your planet, but because your inner life and transformations therein will change your perceptions and expectations of the outer life. Put simply, you are growing out of the playground life. You are maturing spiritually. You are being asked to grow up. Again if I may paraphrase Brother Paul's Hymn in Praise of Love 'When I was a child, I thought like a child, I sought instant gratification like a child, I consumed like a child, I thought nothing of tomorrow like a child; but now I am no longer a child I am done with childish ways.' Dare I suggest that it is no longer even appropriate to think of yourselves as children of God? This change might make more people grow up and take responsibility sooner. From now on consider yourselves as God's Heirs.

And do not be envious of anyone, for it is your privilege to be in the hothouse, even if it does not always feel like that. Your discomfort pales into insignificance when compared to that of your beloved planet, and your decision to volunteer for the Vanguard Army was taken knowing that the training would be a tough one, for such important tasks await you to bring about the victory of Divine Law over human law. Think what heat and pressure that lump of coal must go through to become that sparkling diamond. Would you not want it to do so? And for those who are in the greenhouse, the heat and pressure is on!

And so as much of the human race advances in pursuit of physical comfort and meeting· of material needs with considering the consequences, so the effect of such upon the planet demands that souls like you are willing to transform and mature under the intense glare of the Cosmic Sun in order to keep a few steps ahead so that the scales are always tipped in favour of evolution. The heaviness of the path as you sometimes feel it, with its accompanying tiredness and battle weariness, is hardly surprising when you consider that you are hauling up much of mankind behind you.

Undoubtedly some of you have lived lives where you have played a part in the construction of great temples; I do not mean as architects but as labourers in the sun, moving great weights. But you know, in those early days they, you, knew how to transport great weights as easily as if it were paper through the power of mind over matter. Such gifts are still available to you, although I do not mean now in the sense of physical weight.

My reason for reminding you of this is so that you do not feel burdened by the concern over what appears to be the destruction of your planet and the suffering it brings to your fellow humans. Many of the compassionate ones amongst you cannot help it. We see these issues preying on your (un)conscious minds, even though you may not have made the connection between this and the fluctuation in your sense of well-being. We certainly do not want you to be less compassionate, but that your compassion can be reinforced by a degree of detachment and trust in the higher plan unfolding.

In your quiet time, as you enter within the temple of your heart which you have already so beautifully constructed, imagine the raising up of consciousness upon your planet as being as easy as lifting a huge rock with the tips of your fingers. In so doing you will rise your own vibration; you will bring lightness into all your interaction with others; you will not feel weighed down; you will trust more and more in the Divine power within you so that, most importantly, you will not be deterred from any task, no matter how heavy it seems.

I would like to say one more thing about the greenhouse. The plants within it not only enjoy perfect growing conditions through the intensity of the light, but also from the extra care of those whose task it is to encourage the rich harvest. In that sense, Dear Ones, we your guides see to your needs. From the tenderest seedlings to the full grown, we protect you with the commitment of a parent with a child a thousand fold. Rest assured, in spite of the occasional discomfort, doubts and disillusionment, you will not go without.

My Dear Friends, God's Heirs all of you, you shall inherit the Earth, and be blessed.

19

WHAT IS PAST

YOU KNOW, Dear Ones, it does no good to mourn the passing of civilisations and races of people. All of life is an evolution and anything that is unwilling to evolve must eventually destroy itself; destroy itself that is in its physical form for many of you have had lives in civilisations that no longer exist but you are still very much alive as I might add am I, albeit without a physical form.

To take a contemporary example, you are right to hold in your prayers the people of Tibet as they undergo their suffering but the religion of Tibet had become like a luscious fruit on a tree that was in danger of shrivelling up so it had to be cut into so that the juices could flow towards you so that you may be nourished by it. So nothing has been truly lost but your world has gained much from the sharing of this rich resource of spirituality that was once jealously guarded behind mountain ranges.

By all means continue to express your compassion and solidarity with those who have suffered but without judgement, for this has been their soul's choice as much as it has been yours to be born into your circumstances. You could do much to help their cause and your own by looking at what you can gain from the knowledge and wisdom now available to you instead of regretting what has happened to make it available. Ask yourself even if it is possible that one part of the suffering of the Tibetan people is the price they have agreed to pay to share their riches with you! Can you imagine a world without the compassion and wisdom of the Dalai Lama available to you in books and talks?

There may be other such great souls now living in isolation in your jungles whose isolated existence until now has fostered a connection to God that needs to be shared amongst you all as has what came out of Tibet. There may be an anthropological price to pay if this is to happen but if there is to exist a Brotherhood of Man then all human beings need to be embraced in it and none can live in isolation from their fellows for ever.

Dear friends, does an apple tree mourn the loss of its leaves in Autumn? No, because it knows that without it there could not be new growth and a new harvest; it looks forward to that; it trusts in the cycle of nature as designed by God. The tree lives on through many seasons. So does the soul of man. Civilisations may come and go, like the leaves on the trees; each leaves behind a legacy to enrich your world as the rotting leaves enrich the soil at the base of the tree that it may grow taller and stronger.

So, give thanks for all that is past, as the tree gives thanks for the decaying leaves that feed the soil in which it grows. As the energy of the old leaves is in the new growth in Spring, so the energy which lives on from past civilisations, in the experience of your own soul that lived there, in the wisdom spilled from the falling cup, feeds your growing now. You do not have to look back for the best of the past is in you now and around you now. Let go of the past and know without a fraction of doubt that all is perfect now.

20

KINDNESS

I HAVE a dream, and my dream is that one day all your world leaders, and by that I do not mean political or religious leaders as you now have, but true leaders, your true representatives, will come together to make a momentous decision.

And the decision they will make will be that Mankind can no longer be called by that name but from that time on they will be called Kindman. And from then on your planet will be known throughout the Universe as the planet of Kindness.

Kind men, women and children, I urge you to start that process now that my dream may manifest as soon as possible. Express kindness everywhere to everyone and everything. What a glow that will bring to your heart, immediately that you start, for your heart responds to kindness as the rosebud responds to the warmth of the summer sun.

Try to live as much as possible by Divine Law so that human law can become redundant. From now on know without a shadow of doubt that the source of all your good, the meeting of all your needs at every level is from God alone, for kindness can only be truly expressed when it is given freely and that is difficult when you are experiencing lack or fear because you have given the power to provide to something outside of you.

Live in Divine time, where everything happens at the perfect time so that you can live confidently in the now, knowing that all is perfect with your life every minute of every day. You cannot express kindness truly when you are stressed or because you are worried about being late, for kindness requires that you be in the now with the person you are being kind to.

Build a temple in your heart where Truth may enter in so that your churches and temples where you go to be controlled by false beliefs of punishment and judgement may become redundant also. If it had been Jesus's intention for churches to be built in His name He would have spent His life on earth cutting ribbons. He expressed his kindness in the highways and byways of life, from his Christed heart, without judgement or exclusion. Kindness needs to be expressed unconditionally, indiscriminately but always respectfully and never forcibly.

The more of you who have the courage to live upwards in this way and to put your trust in Truth alone, the more those structures that succeed in ruling your life by fear and misuse of power will begin to crumble. It will include your governments, your religions, your legal systems, your financial houses, and anywhere else that you have invested your energy in any form.

The new leaders who will emerge will have been endowed with authentic power by having been anointed. They will be the ones most perfectly embodying the Truth at that time and who have agreed in their souls to take on this task. They will not be motivated by personal ambition and because they will have all been invested with the same power, the power of Christ Love, there will be no competition or division amongst them, nor any clash of ideals for they will all be serving the one goal. Nor will they try to hold on to their power and as more and more of you become similarly anointed so responsibilities for decision making will be shared, each will know their task, like the original disciples. Remember, the leader amongst them after the Master had left was always the Holy Spirit that unified them, not an individual. And so it remained amongst the early Christians for three centuries.

Can you remember those days? Some of you may have a feeling that you lived in the region of influence of those first Disciples. You would be right which is why the name of Jesus moves you so much now, as much as it did when you heard his name spoken with such love by those who had known him personally. It is like hearing the name of a long lost friend who has come back into your life. For many of you it was in that life that you made your commitment to serve the Christ in this life now. Your lifetimes since then have taken you on many a perilous and painful journey to bring to your soul now the resources of love and wisdom to equip you for the task of helping mankind to become kindman. If those intervening lives have been the years of study, it is in this life that you will graduate from God's School of Love.

21

YOUR LARGER
PURPOSE

You often talk about the larger purpose that some of us are aiming towards. Is there a way we can discover what our larger purpose is now?

IN A general sense, yes. Simply put, the first purpose of your presence in a physical body now is to evolve spiritually, for its own sake, not because it is leading you towards fulfilling any task but that the desire for a closer relationship with God with all that it promises to bring is paramount. To that end you have chosen certain circumstances such as where you were born and through whom to provide a basis for that journey. Many have found, and still find, that that alone is a large enough reason for living.

But I would rather answer your question in the context of this specific time in the history of your planet and humankind. So I would say that your reason for being born now is threefold.

Firstly it is to be a witness to the great changes now taking place upon the face of your planet, especially in terms of human consciousness. This explains your population explosion and why there are so many souls currently incarnated because it is about the most exciting time in mankind's history for a very long time. You are all cramming in there to be a part of it and to make the most of circumstances on Earth now for your evolution. Who does not want to be a part of history in the making?

Secondly, for many of you the choice to be born at this time is to avail yourselves of what is currently available to help you specifically on your journey, perhaps from those who are a little more advanced than you are.

Thirdly, and most importantly you are incarnated now to make your own special contribution towards these changes, to be a part of the Vanguard Army which will march forward holding the white flag proudly aloft, a white flag not of surrender to an enemy, but of those who have surrendered their lives to the will of God.

But where we see many of you making a mistake is in the belief that to feel yourself a part of this Vanguard Army you have to be seen now through what you do as being involved in this movement. Already we see many dear friends suffering because they believe that to serve you have to train as this alternative practitioner or another with the result that they are waiting in their consulting rooms for the patients who are sitting in their consulting rooms waiting for them. While we celebrate any calling to help another, we also want it to bring fulfilment, not stress about how you can pay the bills.

Dear Ones, you are human beings, not human doings or human havings, and your greatest contribution will be made by who you are, not what you do, and your beingness is a part of you that never switches off. I am sure you will have known people who made you feel better, not by anything they said or did, but from just being with them. Would you not like to know that you were having exactly the same effect on people everywhere you go, not just in the work place but also in the highways and byways of life? In that case your doing is born out of your being, whether it is talking to someone sitting beside you on a bus or massaging the person on your table. This is not to belittle the beautiful effect a massage can have but to let you know that the experience of the person receiving it is enhanced by the power of your beingness, not your skills alone. There is a limit to the degree to which you can develop your skills, but there is no limit to the development of your beingness.

Are you reluctant then to talk about someone's life purpose in terms of a specific job?

If I am allowed to I will spill as many beans as there are to spill, but if I were to tell you that your task was to do X you would put all your energies into that and may even accomplish it, but you might then not go beyond that task and in truth there is no limit to what you can do. Even Jesus said, the things I am doing, you can do the same, and more! Now that was not a wind up; He did not do all that He did to show how clever He was; in saying this He wanted to inspire all who believe in the power of the Christ Love that through that Love all things are possible. It is not saying also that you need to heal and perform miracles as He did to successfully fulfil a life purpose, for whatever you do with Love is going to be good, only that you do not allow your conditioned mind or false modesty to limit what is possible for you to accomplish.

Remember Jesus did not say 'I am nothing', he said 'On my own I am nothing'. There is a big difference. If you look only to your human capabilities you will not fulfil your potential, but by entering through surrender into a co-creative relationship with God, you can do as Jesus did.

It is human to want to provide labels for yourself so that when someone asks you what you do you can say with pride 'I am a doctor' or 'I am an artist' or whatever. A far better response to such a question would be to say with confidence and joy. 'I don't know really; I just am.' Make that your goal!

The truth is that whether you are now active in working for others or not, you can do no better than desire to live a life of love in action and that is something you can do any minute of any day. Whatever your future task is, it is inevitably going to involve the heart so why not start getting into practice now like an athlete prepares for a race. Many of you imagine lives of service for yourself that will put you in a spotlight but you cannot be truly ready to serve in such a visible way until you are happy to do so in a way that nobody sees. Part of your training to take on the larger purpose of your life is in the attention to the little acts of service that are there to be done at any time. Start by expressing your love through sacred intention, perhaps by every time you light a candle it for someone; and of course every time you blow it out send the light to someone. Never waste light! If you look for it you can find countless ways each day of expressing loving kindness, to your fellow humans, to animals, to the plants in your garden; then you can help to fulfil my dream of humankind changing its name to kind human.

22

WHERE DO
YOU BELONG

SOME OF you believe that you do not belong to planet Earth, that you come from some other place in the Universe and you long to 'go home'. You see your existence in a human body as being 'on loan' to Earth for a while as she goes through her transformations and that you can then go back to Sirius or the Pliades or wherever it is you consider to be home.

What I would say is that it matters not where you come from in all the Universe, because you come from the same God, the same creative force whether you are an Earth Being or a Pleidian or a Martian. So I would say that anyone who is feeling such homesickness has missed the point of their true origins and that such a feeling is pointing to a belief in separation from God, the spiritual home, rather than a planetary home base. Coming home is coming to the realisation of your Oneness with God, wherever you are.

Many of you have of course experienced existences on other planets, as a part of your education you might say, where you would not have had a physical body but that does not account for the discomfort that some of you feel in your human bodies now. One of the lessons of the earthly condition is to experience the density of matter and to find that the way to transform it into something that is light filled is by raising the level of consciousness in your soul.

Matter follows consciousness and all of you contain the potential to transform your bodies into vehicles of light that will allow you to free yourself from the constraints of the physical laws of Earth. It was because Jesus' body was so filled with the light that he could walk on water. This may be possible for you one day too, not to mention being able to travel around your planet without any form of transport, not even a magic carpet. Sounds incredible, doesn't it? And environmentally friendly too! But the body does not follow consciousness instantly yet, and you can thank your lucky stars for that. None of you yet have sufficient control over your thoughts to avoid some embarrassing incidents. Imagine if you are carrying your heavy shopping to the car and wish for a second pair of hands! And what about the times when you wish you had eyes in the back of your head?

The frustration many of you feel is that your body has yet to catch up with your spiritual vibration and so you are even more acutely aware of the contrast between the longings springing from the lightness in your heart and soul and the heaviness of the physical vehicle. Do not be disheartened, Dear Ones, for it is simply not yet the time for your body to be answering the call of your soul. It is not betraying you for it is not there to provide you with an escape route from your frustrations with the human condition, much of which you have chosen anyway, but at the right time it will cooperate perfectly with your soul's mission on Earth. For a time yet it remains your teacher. Make the most of what it can teach you about the wondrous dimensions in which you now live. For example, about the law of cause and effect as it interacts with your emotions; about the pleasure it can receive as you nourish it through your five senses; that not even the seeming limitation of a dense physical body can separate you from the love of God.

Work too at purifying your body further by all the means known to you, so surrendering the toxic residues of old emotional pain as well as what you have physically ingested. All the time keep up with the process of surrendering through prayer in ever increasing faith and trust to the Highest, so lightening yourself of your burdens of fear and longings for the illusory security of the outer world. The combined affect of all of this will eventually lead you to a state of being where what you discover within yourself will prove to be infinitely more alluring than any heavenly body outside of yourself.

More than that, when you reach such a level of being, when all of you resonates with the Truth of God's omnipresence, you will be one with even the dimmest star that you can see in your night sky. You will be linked to it, to all of the Universe by that single Truth making the distance between you an illusion. Direct a thought at any planet and it will be received there as its light reaches you, but much more quickly than your scientists could ever imagine.

So if you are still homesick for your planet you know now that with your thoughts you can be there within the twinkle of a star.

23

YOU ARE A
SACRED VESSEL

IT IS second nature for many of you to 'carry' those whom you care about, and even at an impersonal level to overly identify with the suffering of any part of God's kingdom. This is not helpful either to you or the person who you are 'carrying' if the result is that you become depleted in your energies or even feel the negativity of others as your own depression and sadness. It does no good for the ills of an individual or your beloved planet either if any awareness of these ills leads you merely to state them as a fact.

Remember that to make any statement of fact using the present tense has the same affect as making an affirmation. To state the fact of an unhappy situation affirms its likelihood to perpetuate its presence in your life. To merely state as a matter of fact that so many trees are cut down each year or even will be cut down by a certain date is to energetically sanction that activity and inflame it, the very opposite of your intention. If inferred in the statement is also a judgement against the perpetrator then you inflame the situation more.

Positive action is not in being an armchair activist which serves only to activate the negative energies and separates you from Truth. Then it is not only your fields and forests that are polluted but your own heart too and your words will sound like those clanging symbols and gongs that Brother Paul spoke of as effect of the pronouncement of facts without Love. Nor is victory gained by countering destructive elements by fighting against them with aggression for then you engage them and you enter into a power battle which can never provide a lasting solution. It may also lead you to a greater feeling of impotence and futility that can drain you of even more energy.

Dear Ones do not get me wrong. I do not in any way seek to diffuse your passionate concern for your beloved planet or indeed for any object of your care and concern. We, your loved ones in the world of Light, celebrate your concern and we love you so much for it but I must remind you of the words of Jesus: 'I of my own self can do nothing.' We only want you to come to a point of being able to celebrate for yourselves in seeing positive change arising from your partnership with God and Divine Law in action through you. For that you need to refrain from judgement, to affirm Truth rather than what is true in your world, to forgive those who go against the law 'for they know not what they do', to invest your energy into raising yourself up ever higher to be a more effective vehicle for God to work through you.

In this way you can do so much to support those who have found a vocation now to serve through a caring organisation. If they are the foot soldiers then make yourselves the airborne troops dropping bombs of light on those who go against the creation of Heaven on Earth. In time of course, when all will be wise to the ways of Divine Law, the foot soldiers will be parachuted up to join you. Until such time their paths are unfolding well for them where they are for their intention is the same as yours and it is in their intention that they now grow. Remember, for evolution to occur it does not matter if things succeed or not in Earthly terms if the intention is right and true.

If you do not yet feel fully airborne it is unlikely that you will be immune from the effect of so much caring on your physical and subtle bodies. Some of you even carry in your auric graffiti a message inviting others to dump their worries on you. If you go out shopping one day and it seems as if everyone is knocking into you then they may be dumping as they are bumping. Your invitation may be because of your genuine desire to alleviate others suffering, but unless you also have the purity of vehicle to transmute the suffering then your world is not the better for it. So when moods arise for which you can find no immediate explanation it is wise to ask yourself if indeed that uncomfortable feeling is yours or belonging to someone else. If the answer is 'no' then a firm command to all that is not yours to leave may do the trick. If not try imagining that you are standing under a shower of light that will wash away anything that should not be in your aura.

Such a habit of carrying others' pain may arise from 'training' early in life to be a peacemaker in your family or to divert tension away from those who should be caring for you by caring for them, so you learn to be a receptical for others pain. Although these experiences may well have been a training for the healer in you to be awoken, your healing work does not have to remain as a by product of a childhood need. There may also be amongst you a few healers who have agreed to heal by taking on the pain of others but the idea is not for such a vocation to be to the detriment of your own well-being.

Perhaps it would help you, if you could see yourselves as I see you, as quite another kind of receptical. I see you as a sacred vessel, like a chalice, waiting to be filled with a life giving energy that is unpolluted by the festering of any old wounds, which will ultimately allow you to transmute negative energy.

With this image I want to take you on a journey, into a visualisation where you will learn how to truly unburden yourself and fulfil the task that a chalice should.

But first you must get out some paper and coloured pencils for I want you to give full rein to your creativity by drawing a chalice. This is not an art examination so do not judge yourself as an artist; just do it with love.

When you have completed your picture I want you then to write into the cup the names of all of those who you are carrying. It may be members of your family or patients. It could be a nation of people or an endangered species of animal. And who do you feel antagonistic towards? Who are you talking to in those times of headspeak? They should be in your cup too for surely such impurities have no place in your chalice.

When this is done it is time to close your eyes and once you have found a stillness create a vision of yourself standing beside a stream in which flows crystal clear, healing waters. Can you hear the sound of the water as it splashes over the stones?

76

Now imagine pulling the chalice out of your abdomen, for your propensity to carry others relates to weakness in both your second and third chakras, and empty its contents into the stream. As you do so see the contents being cleansed and purified as it is washed away towards the ocean of healing consciousness. Perhaps you would also like to rinse the chalice in the stream before you begin walking towards its source. As you begin this little journey contemplate the fact that you have just surrendered all those who you were carrying to a higher power. They are no longer your concern.

Now you arrive at the source of the stream where the flow of water gushes from a rock and waiting for you is a magnificent Being bathed in shimmering white light. Perhaps you will recognise this Being. Certainly you will feel their Love for you. Give your chalice to this guardian of the Source and as he fills your cup you can contemplate the infinite reservoir behind the rock from which this stream of life giving water flows.

The Guardian of the Source holds out the filled chalice for you to drink from. As you drink from it your hands touch. As you drink you feel yourself being renewed, restored, refreshed revitalised by the contents of the chalice. You are aware of all impurities of thought being washed away. You are aware of where you once held the chalice in your body being healed of all pain from the past. And the miracle is that no matter how much you drink the cup is always full.

When you have had enough, the Servant of the Light releases his hold upon the chalice and you place it in your heart where it remains overflowing and available for you to drink from whenever you wish.

24

BREAKING
THE HABIT

IT IS hard for you to imagine living in the future in a consciousness of such bliss as you have been told of. It is hard for you even in your lives now to hold on to states of well-being and joy. It is too good to be true, you tell yourselves, and so as sure as anything your saboteur becomes activated and pulls the plug on your new found happiness. Your life then remains a series of ups and downs.

Joy has a very high vibration and if you have not experienced too many extended periods of joy, when it comes you are not going to be able to tolerate it in your body. If all your dearest dreams came true tomorrow they would probably collapse soon after. Just as if you were to put a powerful electric current into a small circuit without a transformer you would blow a fuse or melt the connections.

Dear Ones, you do not realise it but many of you have become so used to living with dissatisfaction and compromise that it has become the norm for you. Imagine you are setting out on a long walk and at the beginning of the walk you get a stone in your shoe. Because you cannot take your shoe off yet you walk in a way that avoids the pain, perhaps walking on the side of your foot and so putting a strain on another part of your body. But by the time you get to the end of your walk it has become so normal for you to walk in a strange way that when you remove the stone to walk normally seems strange. So if you were to wake up tomorrow morning with not a care in the world, with an unconscious healed of all woundedness, you would feel as if something familiar and friendly were missing, so habituated are you to being in a level of pain.

The healing of this habit rests firstly with the imagination, the instrument of the soul, and following on from that work upon your physical body.

First, use your imagination to take yourself to an unspecified point in the future when something that you now desire has become a reality. For example, if it is a relationship that you desire, imagine yourself with all your longing and loneliness as something of the past, imagine the feeling of being in a committed relationship, imagine telling your friends about your partner, imagine how all of this will make you feel and feel it as if it were *NOW* the reality; try to live as much as you can with the feeling that what you desire is *NOW* manifest. Affirm I am *NOW* with my partner, or whatever it is you desire. Remember, *NOW* is the moment of creation; as you think and believe now, so you will become. Hold on to this feeling as much as you can. As you do so the vibrations of your body will change, they will go faster according to the degree to which you can imagine that joy. As your body gets used to vibrating in harmony with the energy of joy, so the circumstances that can provide that joy in the outer world can be attracted to you. Joy attracts joy. It must happen for it is the law. As within, so without.

Jesus put this very succinctly. He said 'When you want something pray for it and, believing that you already have it, it will be given to you.' Not it may be given to you if God feels like it that day or if you are a good boy or girl; no, it *WILL* be given to you. And believing that what you have asked for is already yours means being in the consciousness *NOW* as if it were there.

So you are then happy anyway and are willing to allow God to bring you your desires in the fullness of time, the perfect time. Remember, God is never late!

And besides, how can anything be too good to be true when the Truth is perfection anyway?

25

BUT IS IT
MEANT...?

IT IS wise not to jump to conclusions when something goes wrong in your life that it must therefore be meant. That is too simple.

If, for example, you miss your train and would not be able to get to an appointment, do not immediately assume that you were meant to miss the train. What is much more likely is that you were meant to be more punctual.

If however as a result of missing the first train you got a later train and found yourself sitting next to someone who transformed your life then you could say you were meant to miss the first train.

The lesson is therefore to look to the long term consequences of what takes place and from that you can deduce if it were meant or not.

26

THE LAST IN
THE LINE

SOME OF you worry about your ego and getting an inflated sense of your own importance as your spiritual growth allows more wonderful things to happen through you.

But all you have to do is to remember that you are the last link in a chain, albeit the only one in a human body, which includes your higher self and at the other end of which is the Godhead.

So when Grace reaches out to someone through you, if they thank you then just imagine passing the thanks back down the line. This way you will remind yourself that good only comes through you, via your higher self.

And your passing on the gratitude will keep the links in the chain strong.

27

YOU ARE LIKE
A SEED CRYSTAL

IF FROM time to time you feel dejected and despairing for your planet when you hear of all that is still being done to harm her, or indeed when you hear of any activity carried out by a fellow human that offends your sensitivity, remember this! You contain within you the capacity to affect change in the consciousness in anyone. The sickness in the soul or sickness in the body of any other human being can be healed by the strength of your spirit.

Think of a seed crystal and the perfect order of its molecular structure. If you immerse that seed crystal in a crystalline liquid it will grow not into any haphazard shape but into a larger version of that original perfect form.

Just as the liquid is latent crystal so all human consciousness is latent enlightenment. If you can see yourself, as being like that seed crystal you can understand it becomes possible for you, immersed as you are in the society in which you live, to generate change in the consciousness of those around you; that as your beingness becomes more filled with light so the disease in those whose energy fields you touch can be healed as they replicate your energy.

Of course it follows that the opposite is also true; your aggressive energy will fuel the same which is latent in others; your negative expectations and beliefs will be acted out by others. Basically, the world will always dance to your tune. And the same applies to your immediate life as well as the world as a whole. Every human response follows the direction of your baton which in turn follows the direction of your beliefs. It is your choice whether you wish to conduct a discordant dirge or a melodious and uplifting symphony.

You will rarely be made aware of the exact affect you can have on others in a positive sense, for you cannot have an effect if your motive is to be rewarded by praise and gratitude from those whom you have helped. The power to transform can only come when you have gone beyond any such ego desires. What you will be aware of as you begin to be able to have such an effect is a sense of joy in living, a deeper understanding of the nature of unconditional love and what it means to live it, a feeling of awe at the wonder and perfection of it all, a heart that overflows with thankfulness and praise and above all an unshakeable love of God.

So how do you bring yourself to that point? Let us go back to that crystal and I would like now to use a diamond as an example for you are that precious to us. As you will know a diamond is very, very hard. No human possesses the strength on their own to manipulate its form. To have an impact upon your world as you would like demands that you become just as strong and inflexible in your adherence to Truth and as resistant to manipulation by human will as that diamond is. It requires that you reflect light as beautifully as any diamond can. In short you need the courage to be to your human world what a diamond is to the mineral world.

Every mined diamond is a latent sparkling gem. Some of you resist the idea of shining so brightly, maybe for fear of your ego running rampant or of being thought by others to have an overblown ego. But Dear Ones, you are all diamonds anyway; you cannot avoid the fact that having prayed 'Thy Will Be Done' you have presented yourself to God as raw materials to be cut and shaped according to His will so that His light may be most beautifully reflected through you. If you give yourself to Him you automatically give yourself to the experiences of life that He uses to bring about the multi-faceted being that you are praying also to become.

It does not mean that you have to be ostentatious in your demonstrations of service. The sparkle does not have to be revealed through an extrovert personality although your eyes will most certainly gain a twinkle. Some may remark that you have an aura about you but such an aura does not easily lend itself to analysis so do not be tempted to do so. We make this analogy only to underline the need for strength,purity, surrender and above all humility, to become effective transformers of human consciousness.

It only takes one person, if what they are carrying is virulent and contagious enough, to begin an epidemic and there is nothing more catching than Love. I call all of you, to begin an epidemic in your area, beginning by doing all that you find necessary to liberate your hearts and minds from all fear and lack of trust so that you are no longer in the thrall of the illusory three dimensional world. This is what Jesus meant when he exhorted his followers to be 'in the world but not of it'. As you then open yourself to experience miracles and grace flowing easily through all of your life so your heart and mind can become bound up in the spirit of celebration and praise which is contagious in itself. But more than that Love enters in, and Love loves through you, and you love Love in return and your love for Love overflows into all of your beingness and your heart knows only one response.

This is when you can walk into a crowded room and the atmosphere changes for the better. This is when you can be standing behind someone in a queue and their headache vanishes or their mood lifts as they receive a vibrational lift from proximity to your beingness. This is how the best in people is elicited and otherwise tense or aggressive situations are healed. This is how peace and goodwill can spread among groups of people and among nations.

Then you will truly understand the words of Brother Paul 'I may know all things and be able to speak in the tongues of men and angels but if I have not love it counts for nothing.'

And the next time you hear somebody saying 'What's the world coming to?' you will be able to tell them with absolute conviction 'It's coming to a beautiful place.'

28

SURRENDER

'BUT I thought I had already surrendered' one of you will say to me when I suggest such a course of action. Worse still for you, will be if, having surrendered, I then say to you 'Be patient, Dear One!' That remark always causes a very interesting reaction in your energy field.

In the first case it will be clear to me that you have not really surrendered because either you are still worrying about it, or you are surrendering your problem every day (as if God needs reminding!) or you are attached to the outcome.

You have not surrendered if what you have surrendered is still causing you to fret. This is the whole point of surrender, Dear Ones, that you give over your problem so that it is no longer your concern and you can then relax. When the problem comes into your mind you can simply breathe a sigh of relief and say to yourself: 'How wonderful that it is no longer my problem and that God is bringing a more perfect solution than I could ever dream of!'

You have not surrendered if you do it more than once, just as you do not have to pray for something more than once. I promise you, Dear Ones, God got the message the first time. There is no set formula or wording to surrender so you do not have to worry that maybe you did not do it properly. It is the sincerity of your intention that counts.

If there is something that you very much want surrendering your desire does not mean giving over to God the responsibility of bringing it to you according to your wishes, as many of you try to practice. I am sorry, Dear Ones, but surrendering your desires can be a risky business for what you are then doing is saying to God 'well this is what I want but if You want to give me something else that you consider better, or even nothing at all, that's okay by me.'

Before you surrender anything, a problem or a desire, I suggest you imagine the worst possible scenario as far as your ego is concerned and imagine living with that outcome. You will in this way heal the fear of such an outcome for surely you will find in imagining it that things will not be as bad as you fear. Above all I hope you will come to the sure realisation that nothing, but nothing, can separate you from the love of God and what could count more than that? Indeed what could be a better outcome to any act of surrender than to arrive at that Truth?

To those of you whose fear of surrender arises from a need to be in control then see that you are surrendering to the God in you, the all-wise, all-knowing, all-loving part of you.

To those of you whose fear is that God wants something different for you than you yourself seek I say 'you'll grow out of it!' It may need you to be brought to your knees before you find out that Divine Wisdom knows where your true joy lies.

Surrender must be unconditional. Surrender is not a calculated decision to bring about anything specific. Surrender is a fearless act of faith. It asks for no guarantee of fulfilment and your considerations of how, where and especially when can be forgotten about.

And do not forget what is to be gained by surrendering your whole life to the Highest. You gain Dominion, which means to enter into a wholly co-creative relationship with the Highest. You will understand the true nature of power for it is only in having learned all that there is to learn about power that your soul will entrust you with so much of it. You will understand fully the meaning of Jesus' words 'I of my own self can do nothing.' You will experience fully that the only true power is Love.

29

SOUL OR SPIRIT

THERE IS often confusion surrounding the difference between your soul and your spirit. I would like to offer you my definition of both.

I would give you the image of a candle within a uniquely and beautifully engraved glass holder. The candle flame is your spirit, the changeless, eternal part of you, the Divine spark within you. The glass holder is your soul; the pattern in the glass contains a record of your soul's experiences so far and a blueprint for what is to come.

If that glass is dirty the flame cannot shine through, no light is radiated, nor can you see clearly the pattern engraved in that glass. You then clean the glass and the more grime that is removed the more light can be given and the clearer the pattern in the glass can be seen. The aim is for the glass to become so clean that the light from the candle is not dimmed by any dirt and the full richness of the pattern is revealed.

It is through the process of evolution that the glass becomes clean. The quality used in the cleaning is the energy of your Higher Self, the all-wise, all-knowing, all-loving part of you. As you resonate with that part of you and therefore use your free will creatively, so more of your light can shine through. Conversely, when you do not listen to that part of you and you use your free will in a way that goes against what you know the glass becomes soiled.

Let your light shine! And as you now know doing just that does not mean that you lose yourselves. Some of my friends fear that if they surrender to the Light to that degree, that they will lose their individuality. The opposite is true; that complex engraved pattern that is the totality of all your lives' experiences as it has enriched your soul becomes even more sharply defined. In it are many hard-won medals for lessons overcome. You have suffered to become the beautiful being you now are so why should such an imprint be erased; cherish and celebrate that rich pattern. You may not be able to feel it or see it for yourself just as when you look at a magnificent stained glass window from the outside you can see nothing. But once seen with the light behind it you are awed by its beauty.

If we continue with that metaphor, each fragment of coloured glass becomes a piece of wisdom gained, a lesson overcome, an act of loving kindness; in its totality it tells the story of your births, your passions, your days in the wilderness, your martyrdoms, your betrayals, your lives of service, your crucifixions and, still to come, your ascensions.

Oh yes, beloved friends, it is all there and we lucky ones in the world of light have the joy to see only this of you. Imagine if you could walk daily through your most magnificent cathedrals with the sun shining through the windows you will know what we experience when we come amongst you.

30

WHO ARE
YOUR GUIDES?

Can you tell me how I can establish a better connection with my guides?

I WOULD rather not! I have to confess I am not terribly interested in guides, even though I am one myself. Nor do I think to do so would be doing you a great service. You do not need to be in contact with them, only to know that they are there, helping you, guiding you and that you are never alone. The current obsession with guides is in danger of becoming a distraction from the true path, for our relationship with you is but a poor substitute for the one that you have yet to establish with your inner guide. You would do far better to put your energy into your journey towards oneness with that source of love and wisdom, however you call it, than to worry about who comprises your back-up team. While you pursue that course of action we will be there, holding the ropes for you until you are able to stand on your own.

What I wish for you is that you will succeed in that so well that you will come to a point when you will be able to say to your guides 'Well boys and girls, it has been wonderful knowing you, whoever you are, but I don't need you any more!' Then we, who are your guides will then be free to move to higher levels in service to mankind and you can take over our jobs on Earth. Would you not like that, to be yourself a guide but in a physical body? When you can make that contact with your 'still, small voice within' you will have access to just as much wisdom and knowledge and love as any guide, perhaps even more.

And in the years that are coming when the pressure will be on for human consciousness to transform itself, there are going to be so many confused and frightened people who will be seeking that sort of help from a fellow human. Not everyone is going to be believing in an old spook like me but they may be very happy to experience your loving physical presence in their time of need, to be inspired by the evidence you provide of the possibility of embodying so much Love and to be healed by it. This task constitutes for many of you the larger purpose in your life and as one who has already fulfilled such a task I can thoroughly recommend it. And I too long to be made redundant.

What would you recommend to those people who are already in contact with guides? Should they forget about them?

No, not at all. It may be indeed that soul's chosen task to act as an instrument but there is a risk of laziness or spiritual complacency setting in when a relationship with a guide is fruitful or meeting some other psychological need. Taking further steps along the path of spiritual growth may lead to letting go of that relationship, just as it sometimes means in your human relationships, or at least a change in the workings of it. Remember, being able to communicate with a guide is not in itself a measure of evolution any more than a dis-incarnate entity's ability to communicate with you is a measure of its spiritual credentials.

There can unfortunately be an element of glamour surrounding guides, even competition sometimes. For that reason I tend to avoid answering questions about the identity of guides because to us in spirit names do not exist in the way that they do on Earth. When I withdraw from my instrument I am no longer White Bull. Imagine also if you were to ask me the identity of your guide and I were to tell you that he had the identity of an Egyptian High Priest you would be a bit chuffed. But then if a friend of yours asked me the same question and I told him his guide was a Chinese peasant farmer he would say 'It's not fair, your guide is an Egyptian High Priest and mine is only a peasant!' But perhaps what I did not tell your friend was that in another life that peasant farmer was an Egyptian Pharaoh. So you see

90

the identity of a guide means nothing; it represents, as my name does, only one of countless incarnations that the guide has had on Earth. I come to you with the name of White Bull only because it was my name in my last life and I need some identity for you to connect with. You can call me what you like really. Whatever name you give me it would not change my message.

There do seem to be an awful lot of American Indian guides around. Why is that?

Yes, I know there has been a fashion for us and now it has moved on. I understand if you want to be really 'in vogue' you must have an extra-terrestrial as a guide.

As I said, I have chosen to be known as White Bull only because it was my last incarnation, not because it was the most notable in terms of human accomplishment. But as you will have noticed I do not limit my teachings to just the philosophy of the Native American although I will draw upon wisdom gained from that incarnation as much as any other I have had.

And there is much that your civilisation can learn from the philosophies of the Native American, much that is urgently needed now to help restore balance to your planet and I hope that at the very least the identity of White Bull will be a reminder of that. But there is also a need to be selective in terms of what is appropriate to be translated into your way of life from my people then.

I would urge you all to make a light study of the ways of the indigenous people such as the Aboriginals of Australia, or the Bushmen of Africa but specifically in relation to their understanding of man's relationship with the Earth Mother and respect for all of Divine Creation and how to live in harmony with your environment. That is what you need above all now and the principles that governed these races in this respect apply no less now. But please do not let such study lead you to mourn the passing of such civilisations or to have your life aroused by the seeming injustices inflicted on such peoples. To do so is to separate such people from the perfection of Divine Order and to hold you in the discomfort of judgement and times past. Nothing is lost. Neither put any past civilisation on a pedestal. When I scan through all my lives on Earth, even as White Bull, I blush at what I got up to. It was so far removed from Truth. There may have been much that was impressive about Ancient Egypt for example, or the Mayan civilisation, but if any of you were around at that time then I can assure you you are infinitely more evolved now than you were then. Perhaps those civilisations had access to knowledge that is lost to you now, but it was not a very hearted civilisation. You, Dear Ones, have love and that is going to serve you far more in your lives now than solving the riddle of the Sphinx or getting your head around the esoteric meaning of the pyramids.

31

TEST THE SPIRITS

YOU NEED to be aware of the fact, Dear Ones, that just because a spirit is living in a world beyond your physical one does not make it automatically a fount of wisdom that you should pay attention to, no matter what their name is.

Dare I say that some of you are a bit snooty about the spooks you keep up with. You swallow the message, hook, line and sinker because of who the messenger is. But just as there are those amongst you who, given the chance, would love to play being a King for a day, so there are some beings in spirit with an identity problem who would leap at the chance of being Napoleon or an E.T. for an hour, not to mention a biblical figure. Yes, there are egos in the astral world.

I say this to you, to remind you that it is the message that counts, not the messenger. The more elevated the source of the message, the more it must be tested whether it is 'of God'.

A message that comes from a place of Truth and Love will not induce fear by predictions of doom and gloom because 'perfect love casts out fear'. A true Messenger of God will bring you 'the good news' that will raise you up, that will empower you and convince you of your ability to contact your Divine Self; it will not command allegiance or guide you towards attitudes that put you in a superior position to others, for God loves all equally and wants all to ascend, now if it were possible. It will not massage your ego but it will encourage you and you will feel seen by it in the depths of your being, wherein lies the glorious, loving self.

A True source will not seek to deprive you of your Divine Right to create your own reality by making predictions for you different from the fulfilment of your greatest potential. A true source will reflect back to you the fact that you are already perfect as you are even without fulfilling your greatest potential.

In communication with a true source you will not be fed by the words alone; deeper than the language of words there is the language of love. Let love speak for itself.

And it is true that there are great masters reaching out to humanity through human instruments, including your favourite saints and even the Master Jesus Himself. But if, for example, you were invited to attend a lecture given by a Master channelled through a human instrument you would experience only a part of that Master's energy. For a human instrument to be able to contain the full energy of a Master they would themselves have to possess the energy of a Master, in which case what would be the point of them channelling anything other than their own power.

And there are servants of the light working for humanity from the spirit world who have no place in your history books, at least not in the identity they give to you, nobodies with no body! But their message need be none the less for that.

Do not forget either the work that is taking place to help you which you will never be aware of because it is done in silence. Countless beings are helping you, our dear friends on Earth, to reach your Promised Land, leading you out of your exile in the land of fear and lack and separation towards that state of Heaven on Earth. They seek no recognition; they serve for servings sake and because they love you more than a human mind and heart can ever comprehend. Their reward is in the joy they find in that.

And so it is on Earth, that there are those of you whose life of service will lead you to positions of prominence in the public eye and there are those whose work will be confined to the highways and byways of life. But the one who becomes famous does not gain more spiritual brownie points than the one who serves in the background. It is the spirit in which the service is performed that brings the reward and just as the famous one runs the risk of believing himself important, equally the unknown server runs the risk of false modesty. Neither of these reflect authentic empowerment.

Still more of you know little about service, but what a wonderful surprise awaits such friends when they arrive in the spirit world and they can review the life they have just completed.

Imagine the scene. One of you arrives in the spirit world and one of the Masters of Karma will say to us 'Who will help this dear one review their life?' And we all put our hands up trying to catch his attention, saying 'Me, please! Please, Sir, me!' And the reason we love this job is to watch the joy and wonder come over you as you discover that a life which you thought achieved nothing was in fact filled with many little acts that came to you so naturally you did not even think about it as service; they were acts of spontaneous kindness performed with the purest love that could come from you.

The lesson in this is that it is not for you to even begin to judge or measure your or another's contribution because there is no human yardstick for it. Just keep on doing the best you can with the gifts you possess. With these gifts there is nothing too high for you to achieve and there is no task too menial that if it is performed in the right spirit cannot bring you to the same heights.

32

PROPHESIES

YOU ARE being bombarded at this time with many different prophesies relating to the future of mankind and your planet.

I want to remind you that one of the oldest prophesies of all is that there will be many false prophets. There has been no time since that prophesy was made when its message has been more relevant than now.

We see confusion amongst many of you, not only because some of the predictions contradict one another, but also because you fear the consequences of not heeding the warnings that they contain.

Amongst the many predictions now reaching you through material channelled from spirit, there are those which are untrue or distortions of the truth.

Understand, Dear Ones, that the methods available for spirits like myself to reach you are always going to be imperfect means of communication, but at the moment there can be no other way. Our work with you is a development in the relationship between our two worlds that began a few decades ago with what you call your spiritualist movement. As time has gone on more refined but less spectacular contact between us has been made. You no longer need the theatricals of physical medium-ship such as transfiguration and ectoplasmic manifestation to convince you of the reality of the spirit world although we encourage a healthy scepticism when meeting spooks such as myself. Gullibility is to an astral entity what the smell of blood is to a shark. It is a rare human instrument indeed who is able to maintain sufficient objectivity, humility and spiritual health to be always the perfect channel.

It is our desire that you will benefit from the teachings we bring you, but it is also our desire that you will learn the lessons of discernment and discrimination as you go about selecting that which is true for you amongst the plethora of channelled information.

But what we desire most of all is that your journeys of evolution will take you to a place of such trust in your inner voice that you will rely on it alone to bring you the information needed to live fully in the now, without fear of the future, and to be guided by it spontaneously, every minute of every day. This is the perfect communication. As St. Paul has said in his hymn in praise of Love 'When the perfect comes, the imperfect will be superseded.' Then I can retire and draw my pension! And you can throw away this and every other book you have!

Until such time as that inner connection is made and you are still stuck with the likes of me you can learn the lessons of discernment. One of the best ways to do this is to use your body.

Your body cannot lie. You can easily train it to respond to Truth in the same way that it responds now to good news after a period of tension. Your lungs will want to take in more air as your whole being wants to receive the life force into it as at that point life is perfect. The Truth is also perfect. You may also find your back straightening and your head being raised as all of you is drawn upwards and you feel perfectly poised between heaven and earth. Or you might feel a tingling or have goose flesh. These are your verification signals. These signals are your body ringing true to the Truth you are reading or hearing.

You may feel this with only one sentence out of a whole book or with all of its contents. Whatever, do not fear rejecting those parts that do not ring true with you.

If you can do this you will ensure that you will not be carried away by some New Age faddism, you will be charting your own course and you will bring yourself nearer to that place of authentic empowerment when all of you sings in glorious harmony with Truth.

33

MORE ON
PROPHESIES

WE, YOUR guides and angels and loved ones in the world of light, observe many troubled hearts in our friends on Earth as you contemplate the consequences of some of the predictions made for your planet.

Especially troubling for many of you is the interpretation given to the calendar of an ancient civilisation which could not see beyond the first decade of your third millennium. It has been taken to mean that life on Earth as you know it will no longer exist after that time and that only a select group of people who adhere to your New Age beliefs will be saved to birth the new order.

Dear Ones, if you are one of those who believe you will be saved you might be rather disappointed to know that the same belief is held by followers of other belief systems too. How would you feel if you had to share your patch with a few Christian and Islamic fundamentalists? All the problems that these changes had occurred to put right would start all over again; there would not be that glorious brotherhood of man that you so passionately seek to found, but the same old divisions and conflicts. Dare I say also that the assumption you will be saved points to a modicum of conceit, as if you know that your way is right.

A shift in consciousness into the fifth dimension might indeed be interpreted as a shift in polarity but it does not have to be of the Earth's axis as has been predicted. Could it not also be a redirection of human thinking? Just as in your current understanding of your Earth's polarity you have two norths, polar and magnetic, but only one is true north, so mankind is divided in its allegiance to false gods and Truth. With the shift into the fifth dimension will surely come that polarisation of the human heart to an alignment with absolute Truth away from the multitude of truths that govern life on Earth right now.

I want you also to know this. The destruction anticipated by this prediction pales into insignificance beside what would have already happened to you through the folly of your ways without the intervention of the non-physical realm. Countless 'disasters' to humanity greater than anything the Earth could produce naturally are diverted daily by us. It would be nothing for us to neutralise in an instant the effect of a nuclear release. I say this to you not to draw attention or praise to ourselves or to chide you, but only to let you know that you are not working alone in this glorious project of transformation upon Earth and that the protection offered to you is not just as individuals but as a whole. The miracles happening daily go largely unnoticed by you of course except when occasionally you find yourselves saying casually 'Isn't it a miracle that such and such has never happened!' or when you begin a sentence with 'It's incredible...' or 'Isn't it amazing...'

I cannot deny that you might come very close to the brink of self-destruction, even to the eleventh hour and fifty-ninth minute, but why should God's big moment come any sooner?

And who do you think really has their finger on the button anyway?

34

EARTHQUAKES

MANY OF the predictions made for your planet in the years ahead include the increasing frequency of earthquakes and other natural disasters.

I do not like the word disaster because it generates fear. I would like it to be removed from your language. What is so disastrous anyway about someone leaving their body and if they should choose to do it in an earthquake or a flood together with others, is that worse than as a result of an illness or a car accident? Until the time comes when all have achieved the level of consciousness when death becomes a conscious decision there will remain a wide choice of ways to leave the physical body, including through 'disasters'.

Think how much nicer it will be when, with peace in your heart, you will be able to announce to your loved ones that you recognise that the time has come for you to leave your physical body. There will be no grieving because all will have penetrated the illusion that death causes separation; there will be only celebration. If only you could remember what it was like to be born you would understand that dying is a doddle by comparison anyway.

And as for earthquakes, you think nothing of giving your body a good stretch when you feel tension in it. Earthquakes are nothing more than a way for your Earth Mother to relieve a bit of her tension. She has always done this and she always will. If it appears to be with more regularity then it may be wise to look at the tension you carry. I am sure you will agree that there is a lot more stress in your modern world than even a century ago. Where does this stress go? When you were a baby you would discharge your tension into your mother's body when being held by her; babies that are always held are always relaxed and floppy. Now so much of your tension is discharged into the Earth Mother.

Do not forget Dear Ones, that your planet is a living, breathing, organism, like your own bodies. You think nothing of referring to your rain forests as the lungs of the Earth Mother, to your rivers as her veins but you can take it much further than that if you understand really how she is reflecting back to you the state of health of the collective human consciousness. Metaphors abound. For the moment I shall stick with earthquakes.

I want to suggest to you that the earthquakes seen by prophets are symbols of something else. They are not only a means for the earth to have a good stretch but they provide a jolt for those people living near the areas where your earth releases her tension. Their foundations are shaken! Inevitable, you may say; what do they expect?

Your belovéd Master Jesus might well have added to his parable about the man who built his house on sand and the one who built his house upon rock something about the man who built his house upon a fault line. When the earthquake came his house fell down because his foundations were not sound.

I put it to you dear friends, that the earthquakes prophesied in the years to come are not of the earth as you expect, but are the essential shaking of the foundations of those whose lives are not built upon Truth.

If your foundations are based upon your relationship with the material world around you; if your sense of self is based upon how much money you earn, what you look like, how big your house is, then these are foundations built on a fault line. When the earthquake comes you must be prepared for it all to fall away.

This earthquake may take place in your personal life, affecting you alone, or it may be one that will affect many people. For example, your financial and business worlds are built on a ground riddled with fault lines. And when the facts that are already known in certain quarters about what really took place in your Holy Land two thousand years ago are revealed, which they will be, you can expect a major earthquake to rock your Christian religion. Many will have their foundations ripped away from under them. At that time those of you who are already living in Truth will need to be ready to stand firm, revealing the Truth that those who have been shaken may recognise it instantly and be saved by it. The Truth, as revealed in you, will set them free. You will lead them out of the exile in the land of fear of judgement into the Promised Land of Oneness with the Father/Mother God. Does this not sound a wondrous task to perform?

Understand, Dear Ones, that all this will happen as a result of the great forces of light now shining upon your planet. None of what must come is designed to bring you harm, only to set you free, and you have already agreed to it in your souls through your decision to be incarnated at this time.

Those friends on Earth who are resisting the inevitable shift in consciousness onto a firmer ground are those who will experience the most traumatic earthquakes. When you know of or hear of anyone who is going through an experience of loss, perhaps the loss of a job or money, of power or status, do not judge their predicament as wrong or unjust. Especially do not see them as victims of negative forces. Have infinite compassion for them, of course, but also celebrate the obvious sign of grace working in their lives to point out the weakness in their foundations that they may then have a chance to rebuild their lives on a foundation of Truth. And do not doubt, that chance is there for them if they wish to take it.

Those who have dedicated themselves to the path of spiritual growth must also expect the occasional tremor in their lives. Suffering is not inconsistent with the spiritual path; it is a passage to freedom from the suffering already there which has given rise to attachments to externals, false Gods. Suffering on the path may also come as a test of faith. Will you start doubting the existence of God as things start not going the way you would like? Do you really mean it when you pray 'Thy Will Be Done?'

35

Disease

Why has AIDS come to affect mankind?

THERE ARE as many reasons for AIDS as there are those who are affected by it. But if I were to speak generally I would say this; one point of AIDS is not how it is contracted or by whom, but the fact that a disease has manifested that is deemed incurable by orthodox medicine. Of course any compassionate human being is going to want a cure to be found but that is not going to solve the larger issue as inevitably another disease will emerge that will pose an even greater threat and be even harder to find a cure for. The message of AIDS, and all other immune related illnesses, is a call to humankind to strengthen his or her sense of self through relationship to the Source, the only true place of safety and therefore, as matter follows thought, supportive of the body's defence mechanisms. If mankind does not do this then mother nature will present him with even more outlandish diseases that will forever be beyond the understanding of the doctors and scientists.

It follows of course that you cannot enter into a healthier relationship with your Source without developing a greater awareness of your environment and your physical body and the laws of nature that govern them. The principal of 'as within so without' can then begin to manifest in your lives, both your personal lives and the community of mankind as a whole.

Of course if you look at those who are most obviously affected by AIDS in your Western society you will find a perfect example of how an experience of separation gives rise to disease. Somewhere in the psyche of countless homosexuals is a belief, imposed by an outdated moral code, that they are at the very least imperfect in the eyes of the majority and at the worst separate from the love of God. Similarly with drug addicts and any other oppressed community. All such groups are subjected to judgement. There is a cruel irony that the actions of such souls that arise out of their pain as a way to find comfort away from such attitudes is what also brings them potentially into contact with AIDS. Drugs and sex can both be used as pain-killers to numb the grief of rejection.

But you know there is also much that is beautiful which is coming out of the existence of AIDS. So much compassion and loving kindness where it did not exist before; so much desire to serve; so much more tolerance; so much giving as well as receiving of love; so many souls who have grasped the experience of AIDS as a way to evolve rapidly in their understanding of God and Truth. Many of these, dear friends, have arrived in spirit wonderfully equipped to serve mankind with all that they have learned; some will do it from spirit and others are zooming back to Earth as quickly as they can to put into action their experience of love, bringing healing to the lives of those they have recently left. Now you know never, ever to judge a life that is not long in your human terms as a waste.

What about illness in general? What does that teach us?

Again I would say that every instance of illness and disease is an intensely personal experience; there may be many factors involved and no two cases will share all the same factors, but essentially all illness and disease stems from a belief in imperfection. If you believe for long enough that you are imperfect, especially unconsciously, and of course then behave in a way to compensate for that feeling of imperfection, then eventually your body is going to have to manifest that belief. Depending upon the nature of that illness and the part of the body where it manifests, there can be found clues to specific beliefs about imperfection, but whatever they are the way to healing is the same dissolving that belief by affirming the Truth, that you are perfect now.

Your poor bodies are going through so much just to react to your beliefs but if you were to affirm a thousand times a day 'I am now perfect' then all the cells in your body will shout 'Yippeeeee! We can now be perfect! We can be ourselves! Hoooraay!' and very soon you will feel better. Try it now! Of course as you are saying it a little voice inside you will be saying 'this is a lot of phooey' but when you state an eternal Truth no sceptical voice can work against it, and eventually that voice will subside.

But I am not perfect. I only have to look at myself in the mirror to know that, or reflect on what I have done in the past, and is it egotistical to think oneself perfect anyway?

Being perfect does not mean that you have to conform to Hollywood aesthetics. Nor does it mean that you have to be a saint on Earth. Furthermore you can tell me until you are blue in the face all that is wrong with you but it does not wash with me. Because I see you as you really are. Answer me these questions. Do you believe in the omnipresence of God?

Yes.

So therefore you believe there is nowhere in all the Universe where God is not, and that has to include in every part of you. In every fibre, in every cell, in every hair and drop of blood. How else could Jesus say that God knows every hair on your head? Because he is in every hair on your head! You cannot say that God is everywhere but stops twenty centimetres from my body. Now, do you believe that God is Love?

Yes.

So Love is in every part of you! Do you believe that God is perfect?

Yes.

So you *do* believe you are perfect! Hmm, you fell for that one!

105

Whatever God is, you are also. It is only egotistical to think yourself perfect if you exclude God from the equation. You are perfect as God is perfect. You are made in the image of God. And can I say also, Dear Ones, it is as you draw closer to the mirror that you see your imperfections more clearly. So it is that as you draw nearer to God your self-image may take a knock or two and you will feel yourself unworthy. I say this so that you are able to see the positive side to developing negative feelings about yourself, that it can be a sign of progress.

So to all my friends who are ill I prescribe the following medicine to be taken at least a thousand times a day 'I AM NOW PERFECT!'

What if it is the right time for someone to leave the physical body. Can such an affirmation interfere with the soul's desire?

No. No matter what the prognosis is, to state such a Truth is always going to be helpful for the soul's journey.

Remember, Truth will set you free. It may be to free you from the pains of illness or to free you from the physical body if that is the freedom you are seeking. And of course when you are free of the physical body you will arrive in the Spirit world as perfectly whole anyway, with no more aches or pains.

There are so many choices of 'alternative' ways of healing available now. Is it time to abandon orthodox medicine?

Not at all. You know, there are countless souls working in orthodox medicine who are doing so as a result of a true vocation. And there are many souls in the spirit world working to help find cures for your diseases that can be brought to you only through orthodoxy. To walk away from such would be to block the growth of many who seek to serve mankind in this way. There are also many souls working in orthodox medicine who have received a calling to help the sick but who have misinterpreted it and instead of becoming healers have followed the only known path to them. You cannot make them wrong for that.

A day will surely come when orthodox medicine will not be required, but to give up the expertise it now offers is foolhardy, even arrogant. What you must keep in mind is that it can only provide the cure; it cannot heal the root cause. That you must find in another way and, as you say, there are many alternatives available to you. What I look forward to is a time when every family contains at least one healer. Every family should have one, as you have your First Aid Kit in the bathroom cabinet.

What you will find happening also is that your increasing sensitivity will make the side effects of chemical medicine more and more intolerable for your body. As you talk of your evolutionary process so much in terms of raising the vibrational frequency of your bodies so it must be to vibrational medicine that more and more will turn. The medicine of the future will be by treatment with gem and flower remedies and with the direct intervention of healing angels. You will come to a level where instead of calling your doctor you will call upon the angels of healing to come to your bedside.

Oh, how we long for that time of cooperation, of team work between our two worlds! And I do not just mean between you and we who are your guides and angels. You will need to consciously embrace in your notion of team work the elemental world, the nature spirits who tend the flowers and plants from which you will make the remedies, the devas of the mineral kingdom, in fact, as they are called by your Native American people, all your relations.

36

YOUR
DEATH WISH

I SEE so many amongst you, dear friends, who in your heart of hearts do not want to be in your physical body. I can understand this. You would much rather be back in the spirit world. The struggle of the earthly life seems so contradictory to what you know deep in you is the true path and to what you expected for this life.

You came into this life for a purpose, one which could only be fulfilled by already having attained a certain level of evolution in past lives. This means your experience of life in the spirit world allowed you to taste more fully the blissful state which is the reward that such evolution brings.

But it is also such an evolution that allowed you to appreciate more fully the beauty and perfection of the divine plan now unfolding on earth and which generated in you a deep longing to return to earth to play your part in it.

You were drawn by such a vision which you could see so clearly from the spirit world that with great enthusiasm you chose to come into a physical body. Of course such an important life required the right timing and choice of parents to be born through. That you accomplished perfectly although your reasoning minds may sometimes doubt it. But when you began to connect with your physical body you lost sight of that vision that brought you to Earth and at that moment your soul and your physical body began their on-off relationship.

It is hardly surprising therefore, my friends that your life is such a struggle. Without a real commitment to life it must feel for you like going forward in your car with the handbrake on, and in a thick fog so it is hard to know where you are going.

You know deep inside you that there is a purpose for being alive now although at the moment you can only have a vague feeling as to what it is. Be reassured, you are drawing nearer to reconnecting with that vision. Think of it this way; when you buy clothes for a child you always buy them too big, knowing that the child will eventually grow into them. Well the you that is living that vision is the self that you are growing into. The potential you feel in yourself for great work, that sometimes others can see also when you cannot, is that clothing, the uniform of a servant of the light, that is not yet manifest because you need to grow some more before you can wear it comfortably. As for every child there are growing pains but grow into it you will and at the moment that it becomes the perfect fit there will come also the moment of complete and happy incarnation within your physical self. You will be glad to be alive. It will be your moment of giving birth to self.

While you are waiting for that moment you are not going to make life easier for yourself by filling your time with things to do or by making dramatic changes in your life because the circumstances are uncomfortable. That is not making a commitment to life; you will only become more conscious of the void because the only real fulfilment can come by connecting to your spirit. Committing to life is committing to Love, accepting your life as it is now, trusting in the wisdom of your soul's choice and rendering all to the will of God. That is what will create the growth spurt, not looking mournfully over your shoulders from whence you came, not looking forward and getting depressed because you cannot see through the fog, but by looking upwards, and seeing the light of Divine Love that illuminates every step of your life, one step at a time.

Dear Ones, physical birth is leaving home, spiritual rebirth is coming home. And so it is said, unless you are born again you cannot enter the Kingdom of Heaven, but Heaven on Earth!

May I take this opportunity to wish you a blesséd and deeply happy Birthday when it comes!

37

HOW IS
YOUR MEMORY?

DO YOU find yourself more and more bemoaning your failing memory and poor concentration? If the answer is 'no' you have something to look forward to.

If the answer is 'yes' I delight in reassuring you that such symptoms are a good sign, just the sort of thing you should be looking for in fact to give evidence of the changing pattern of your brain waves that are part and parcel of raising your consciousness. Do not complain about it, Dear Ones, for it is the fruits of your labour! I must also reassure you that these symptoms will not last.

What you experience as your failing memory is your mind ridding itself of information that up until now has provided a familiar map for you and instead is preparing you to trust in the guidance of the unseen world from minute to minute without concern for the past or future. Contrary to what many of you think the path of growth is one of unlearning, a distillation into its purest essence of your beingness that you may be an instrument of God's love any moment of every day.

It is also serving you to be able to access more easily wisdom gained on your visits to the Halls of Learning during the sleep state and for the ancient wisdom within you from centuries past to percolate to the surface mind. It is in the Halls of Learning, under the tutelage of great teachers, that you undergo a sort of refresher course to prepare you for the lessons and tasks of this life.

If the path you have followed so far has provided you with a fund of knowledge of course you cannot erase it from your mind at will. Be open instead that your path from now on, as you have dedicated it to the Highest, may make that knowledge redundant. It may also be the perfect raw materials for your path but only if you give its direction and use unconditionally to God's will. If your knowledge remains a tool of your personal ambition then for you death will be surely a tragedy. No matter how worthy or philanthropic your ambition may be, when did you last consult God over it? You will find the answer by honestly asking yourself how much you employ your will to bring about the furthering of your ambition or does Grace open the doors for you? And is the fulfilment of your ambition for God's glory or your own?

As for your concentration problems, is it not so that the three dimensional world enthralls you less and less, if it has ever enthralled you? Do you not desire more and more to rest your mind in another place, insulated against the painful realities of the world in which you find yourself living? When you have got the God bug it is easy to allow the promise of that heavenly state to lure you prematurely away from your 3D lives, but that heavenly state within you is still in the making and is not ready to receive you so your mental absenteeism takes you only into an empty space that offers refuge but not reality. It is too easy also to be seduced by the promise of trainings and workshops to provide a short cut, but they cannot, anymore than a pregnant mother can speed up her time of confinement.

The solution is to aim to do all things with consciousness and love, no matter how mundane or difficult. Promise yourself a time each day when you can allow your imagination to transport you to an unspecified time in the future when you are living in that heavenly state. Stay with the feeling that your imagination, the instrument of your soul, brings you for as long as you can. It is not day dreaming or fantasising for they are creations of the mind as an escape route. Imagination is the creation within you now of the state of being you reach out for in your heart.

The reason you tune a musical instrument is to remove the risk of disharmony. Your symptom of poor memory is a part of your fine tuning, the ordering of the cluttered mind with all the risks of your ego, old habits and inflexibility of will deflecting you from the path of surrender.

And if we use the example of an orchestra, one instrument provides the note to which all other instruments attune themselves. If you think of God as providing that pure note then you will see that all your efforts to grow are your striving to attune to Him that you and all mankind may be in perfect harmony with each other. And at this time that leading note is penetrating into more and more of your hearts and wills. In time none will be immune to its beautiful resonance.

That will be when you enter into the final movement of the Divine Symphony, the drawing together of all of humankind to oneness with God's will, the glorious climax of heaven on Earth, the consummation of all things.

38

ABUNDANCE

I WANT to remind you of a story, one that you know quite well. At least, this is my version of it.

One day Jesus was talking to a group of people, five thousand so history relates, and at one point someone in the front row put his hand up and said 'Excuse me Master, we are a bit hungry. Can we have a lunch break please?' And Jesus replied 'Of course, Dear One, let's see what we can find.'

And all they could find were a few fish and a few loaves of bread.

Now if Jesus had been like most of you he would have looked at the fish and the bread and thought 'Oh golly! There's not enough. Help! There's going to be a riot!' But of course he did not. He was not going to be seduced by the material evidence because he knew the truth about the laws of abundance and that there is always enough for everyone. And so there was. Jesus did not think either 'I'll rustle up a little snack just to keep them happy for the time being.' No, he manifested so much that everyone could have a bellyful.

This story teaches two important things.

Firstly it teaches that no matter how little you have, if you are willing to share it with others without fear of your own lack you will always have enough.

Secondly it teaches that if you allow material evidence born out of your beliefs in lack to dictate your reality you will never overcome separation and your lack will remain. Included in the Truth of your Oneness now is your oneness with abundance. There is no Truth in poverty. There is no Truth in lack of any kind but conditioning arising out of cultural or religious mores, an absence of unconditional love as a child, hangovers from past lives, lead you to take your struggle for material or emotional fulfilment as a normal part of life. Wrong, Dear Ones, wrong!

Whatever is lacking in your life, be it a job, or money or love, reveals a belief in you, probably rooted in the unconscious, in lack. You accept the physical evidence as the only reality. So you say 'I do not have...', 'I'm short of...', 'I haven't got enough of...', thus perpetuating that reality. Can you not see, Dear Ones, what a powerful affirmation that it, especially when it is repeated as often as it is. Most of the time you are not even aware of when you are affirming your lack. Be more aware of your thoughts around lack.

So let me offer this as an incentive. One of the best ways you can serve yourself and others is to make your aim to be a good advertisement for God. Think of yourself as part of a huge public relations exercise to promote the benefits arising from being one with God, not through proselytising, but through manifesting Truth in your lives through faith in God's Laws. Who wants to know God if it means being poor? Who wants to know God if it means being lonely or sick? Nobody! All these conditions can be transcended by faith.

There cannot be anything in your life that seems more impossible than was the feeding of five thousand people with a few pieces of bread and fish. It needs only for you to disengage from the conditioned mind that says that physical evidence represents reality, for you to be able to have miracles happening in your life. What are miracles after all other than the unhindered working of spiritual law.

I offer a note of caution, however. By all means stick this story on your refrigerator door but next time you have a party I advise you to hire the caterers anyway or at least to stock up on food and wine. You may not yet possess the faith to manifest a banquet out of the mouldy bit of cheese and the ageing tomato stuck to the back of your refrigerator.

Start small! I am sure many of you have already succeeded in manifesting a parking place for your motor car or a taxi when physical circumstances dictate that it is impossible. The more you practice living by faith, the more your faith is rewarded, then the more you raise yourself up to connect with the infinite resources of universal energy to manifest the larger things. They will come to you not by any logical means but in a package covered in God's fingerprints. So get rid of your calculator on which you work out how much you can afford for this and how much you need for that. When you think in those terms you will only manifest what you have calculated that you need and you will stay in poverty consciousness. You will always have what you need so why bother with the sums?

Whatever name you call your Source, He/She is not in the habit of withholding from you that which will bring you into a state of being which will reflect the nature of the Source. But the Source does desire that your sense of self or happiness does not become based upon the having or the owning.

This means you will no longer have to envy anyone who has what you would like for yourself. To seek fulfilment and well-being is not to enter into a lottery where if you are lucky your wish will come true. Neither fall into the defeatist belief that to go without must be as a result of your negative karma. The last thing God wants for you is to be involved in an endless game of cosmic ping pong. Were it the case that the law of cause and effect were working in your life to deprive you it would only be because when it was triggered you were ignorant of Truth. You are no longer. The Truth can now set you free. Let your instinctive response be always from now on: 'If they can have it, so can I!'

If Divine law were allowed to operate freely there would be enough food for everyone, enough jobs and lovers and money too. There would be no stockpiling because there would be no fear of running short; there would be no greed for there would be no fear of going without. There would not be the divisions of rich and poor because either the rich would feel safe to give to the poor or the poor would have faith to manifest their needs anyway. There will be no need to save for a rainy day and having all that financial energy lying around doing nothing. How much more money will be circulating and doing good instead of gathering dust.

Imagine what it will mean for your beloved planet! You will be able to dispense with the equation that the more mouths there are to feed the more natural resources need to be extracted or the more trees that have to be cut down to provide land for cultivation. At such a time there will not be the fear of loss or the hunger for profit. Economists will become a dying breed. Countless lives that are now run by fear will be freed from this constraint so their hearts will open wider. So there will be more peace in the world.

Finally it must be said that abundance is a state of being, not a state of having; it is a state of being that comes from knowing without doubt that the infinite love and wisdom of the Divine guides and protects you and that all is eternally well with you, in all ways. Experiencing then an unbreakable link to the limitless treasure chest of Love will bring you a lasting sensation that will beat any passing high that may come from being able to buy that new 'toy'. I do not mean that you cannot have that 'toy', only that if you were to lose it you would shed no tears for you would possess the faith to be able to manifest another.

39

GIVING
AND RECEIVING

ONE OF the most precious gifts you can give to anyone is the chance to give to you. One of the most precious gifts you can give to yourself is to discover the equal joy in giving and receiving.

The desire to serve is so powerfully programmed into so many of you that you forget the need for balance. If your impulse to serve arises from the lack of unconditional love as a child and that you only got the love you needed by being good, then your resistance to receiving will be because you do not think you deserve it.

Think of a tree. A tree is following a single law of nature which is to grow towards the light; having established itself in the earth it begins to grow upwards and as it grows so there emerges from the central stem branches which in turn bear fruit, but always the main thrust is the journey towards the sun. The human spirit is also following a single law which is to grow towards the light, the cosmic sun, so it roots itself in a physical body and begins its journey upwards. Its branches which provide the shape that identifies it from another are the life experiences and lessons learned; its fruit is the service to others.

But there is one big difference between the human and the tree. If you put your ear to the trunk of the tree you will not hear it arguing with the Earth Mother saying 'Oh Mother, I am not good enough to receive your energy through my roots'; you will not see the leaves straining to avoid the sun's rays saying 'Oh Sun, we are not beautiful enough to receive your light and warmth'. The tree knows that if it is to grow and bear fruit then it has to receive, receive and receive, through every part of it.

So the next time you see a beautiful tree laden with fruit that can feed many people, remember that fruit is only there because the tree first received.

40

FAMILIES

MANY OF you wonder why you were born into a family where you feel so out of place and where early conditions were so contrary to your needs.

One thing is for sure and that is that you did not choose your family to enjoy a life of cosy, domestic bliss with them. Many of my friends have chosen to be born into families where they feel different, or misunderstood, or have not been able to establish the same relationship with their parents as their siblings have done. You have probably felt that alienation from the moment of your very first breath when you looked around you and you thought 'Uh,uh! I think I've made a mistake. Who are these aliens? They do not seem to recognise me.' But a decision to be born in such an uncomfortable environment has a reason in that it has served to reinforce within your soul the impetus to discover a sense of belonging that is Divine in nature, and not biological, to experience the unconditional love of your Divine Mother and your Divine Father, a love that no human parent could ever be expected to provide. It is your experience of Divine Love that is not only going to heal you of all the pain arising from your choice of family in this life, but also all that is not healed from all your other lives on Earth, and in so doing help you to overcome all experience of separation from all that is your perfect good, all that is God. The realisation of your true belonging is also essential for the larger purpose of this life to manifest. It also follows that when you know who you are in relation to the Divine Parents you will be able to experience a greater closeness to your biological parents and to see them more as fellow souls on a journey rather than in a strictly familial role.

And so it follows that your choice of family, no matter how bad your early life has been with them, has been the best one to bring you onto your path of growth now. You may want to try to find it in your heart to thank them rather than complain about them. Remember, you chose them! And remember too, that they may find themselves with a child that they do not understand, who does not fulfil their normal expectations of how a parent/child relationship should be; this is a painful experience for them and is often the sacrifice that their souls have agreed to make so that they can indeed be the springboard for your larger purpose to begin. And do not forget that whatever difficulties exist between you and them, indeed between you and anyone, while you are arguing with each other and hurting each other with words at a personality level, your souls are enjoying a nice cup of tea together, in perfect harmony with each other.

How can I experience the love of the Divine Father and Mother?

The arms of the Divine Parents are forever held wide open for you to walk into their loving embrace whenever you wish. Nothing ever will stand between you and that opportunity for it is an unconditional love that asks nothing in return.

If it is hard for you to imagine walking into the loving embrace then ask for the Mother or Father to come to you to scoop you up. Ask for it with the same simplicity and trust that a child who trusts its physical father will ask to be picked up and held, or will expect his mother to kiss better his cut finger. It never enters the child's head that he will be refused. Whenever you have a need, that love is there. When Jesus said: 'Knock, and the door will be opened, Ask, and you will receive' this is how He meant it should be done.

It sounds so simple, and it is to one who already has that experience from his or her biological parents. If you have been without it, then it takes practice. You need practice above all in receiving without there being a price to pay. And what, Dear Ones, comes cheaper than the air you breathe? Breathe in the breath of God which contains that Love. It is all around you; every time you breathe in with this thought you are making a powerful affirmation because you are saying Yes to Life!

Yes to Love! Yes to the Father, Mother God! There is no more powerful affirmation than conscious breathing. In time, as you develop the habit of receiving that life-giving energy, which is Love, into you you will want it more and more. And in the wanting, which I hope will turn into a hunger, your own soul will guide you to new ways of experiencing that Love. You know Dear Ones, to feel hunger for the love of God needs to be one of the most beautiful feelings you will ever experience. Pray never to be without it.

So what is the best way to 'honour ones' father and mother'?

First, as I have already said, do not make them wrong because they were not the 'perfect' parents. In all of human history no parent has ever got it all right in human measurement and there is no reason why your parents should have been the first.

Secondly, honour the contract you made with them to be born through them to do whatever is essential for the reason for your incarnation and your journey to unfold, even if it means taking action that you know will hurt them. If you act only to placate their personality selves, then you damage yourself by giving your power to them. Serve the highest in yourself and you will automatically serve the highest in those who are closest to you. At this point let me tell you, or rather remind you of a story.

One day Jesus was visiting a village; a young man, when he heard that Jesus was around, searched frantically for him because he wanted to be a follower. And when he found Jesus he said to him 'Oh, Master, I am so glad I have found you because I want to be one of your disciples and I want to be with you;' And Jesus said 'Well that's great dear one and you find me at the perfect time because I am just about to leave. So let's go!' And the young man said 'Oh, I'm dreadfully sorry, I can't come with you now because I've got to bury my father and my mother!' 'Oh!' said Jesus, 'I'm afraid that is not how it works. If you want to follow me, now is your only chance, do it now; let the dead bury their dead.'

The truth of the story was that the young man's parents were not physically dead as you would normally understand it but they were spiritually still asleep. Their son however had awoken to the truth of Christ Love. Jesus, knowing this, urged him to follow his true vocation, leaving those who had not yet received it to look after each other.

We know what courage it takes to do this, to break free from the mould of society's expectations but as many of you have had past lives spent in monasteries or convents where you would have had to cut ties completely with your family to honour your vocation, you are only doing the same thing now, except this time you are not necessarily being asked to leave your families for another physical place, just for a different place in consciousness from which they too can benefit if they wish.

What do you suggest in the case of an only child who finds herself in the position of caring for an elderly relative? In such a situation it is not so easy to leave the parent in an old people's home just to be able to follow a personal spiritual quest?

In such a case to honour the parent is to heal any basis for resentment towards him or her because personal desires have been thwarted and to accept the situation without having to pathologise or understand it in terms of karmic debt or spiritual lesson. Seen in those terms it becomes an unavoidable duty which must therefore stifle any of your heart's spontaneous desire to expand through love in action. It is important also to free the parent from that one role in your life but to see him or her as a soul pursuing its own unique journey, only a part of which includes having taken on the role of your parent. You might also wish to see it as an opportunity to grow through loving and serving the Christ, the Christ in your parent.

If on the other hand circumstances prevent you from taking a caring role, you will first honour your parent and yourself by not allowing yourself to feel any guilt because of this. Guilt is a synthetic emotion, an idea created by man to give him power over others. When the time comes that you are in the spirit world discussing this life with your guides and you say to your guide: 'Oh I felt so guilty that I did not do more for my father' your guide is likely to say 'Excuse me a minute, dear one, I must go and fetch my dictionary because I do not know this word guilt.'

To serve in the highest way anyone who you cannot be with physically who is in need of care or who you might otherwise worry about is to hold in your mind the highest vision for them, of their radiant, joyous, healed, vital self, that is their True Self, and which they will become when they make their transition. Do not focus upon what you see as the decaying of their physical and mental self, nor upon the limitations of personality that push your buttons, for all that will pass away. The eternal part of them that in this lifetime has been committed to helping you on your journey needs now your recognition, your gratitude and your highest vision.

41

PARTNERSHIP

FOR THOSE of you born into what you call your Western society this may be the first time in a very long time, and by that I mean several hundred years, when you have complete free-will when it comes to choosing a partner. It may be that you were once a part of a culture where marriages were arranged by parents; equally you could have been living in a society that made no allowances for separation or divorce so you would have been trapped in a loveless marriage; it could have been that you would have found it necessary to enter into a relationship merely for reasons of survival, thus forcing you into a situation of endless compromise. Just as likely you chose to make vows of celibacy and entered into a monastic life. But now it is through your experiences of personal relationships that you not only undergo the most intense opportunities for your self-healing but also give yourselves the chance to experience a truly Divine 'marriage'.

When you meet someone to whom you are attracted to you of course want to make a positive impression, but while you and the other person are engaged in the rites of early courtship your aura is ablaze with lights flashing to illuminate the graffiti that reads something like 'I need to be rejected by you to prove to myself that I am ugly' or 'I'm a master control freak seeking willing victim.' So before you have even got as far as discussing your tastes in music you and your new friend have handed each other a detailed list of all your buttons; your rejection button, your control button, your victim button and so on. And the scene is set.

Your choice then becomes when one of these buttons is pressed, are you going to allow it to reinforce that pattern or are you going to say to yourself, 'Oh, how nice of You to point out that I still have buttons to be pressed. Now I have a chance to grow and be healed so that no other person has the power to decide whether I am happy or not.'

This becomes especially confusing for you, when that other person is what you like to call a soul-mate or twin-soul. Of course you want to believe that a soul-mate would never do those things that hurt you so much, but if you also believe that a soul mate is a soul who loves you especially you will understand that he or she is also wanting only your highest good; so sometimes it does happen that one soul-mate will take it upon itself to cause pain to another so that as a way to heal that pain the other will turn towards God. What greater gift of love can there be than to bring you close to God? So look back at all of those who have caused you pain, even those who you may have considered your enemies for they could be a soul mate as well, and see what gift was in that experience of knowing them. At the very least I am sure you will find opportunities to grow closer to God through a true understanding of what it means to forgive. And you will learn something more about compassion too because if someone has acted in a mean way towards you and has hurt you they are only saying in a different way 'Ouch, I'm hurting! Please love me!'

And if you should find yourself in a situation of feeling so deeply a soul bond with a loved one but you are unable to make the relationship work at a human level, do not despair or give up too easily. It may be that your personalities have still to catch up with the souls and this can only be done with persistence and trust and a commitment to be patient with each other and kind to each other. Whatever, give it all over to the highest in both of you to negotiate at a level beyond where your wounded egos may cause problems and delays.

I would only warn you of one thing and that is do not be carried away or intoxicated by the experience of meeting one with whom you feel such a close bond between your two souls. If your inner voice tells you that your relationship has a higher purpose and that your union in this life follows on from many other shared lifetimes more than ever before, you need to remain centred and not to lose yourself in the other; this can only lead to pain and confusion.

You may be disappointed also if you try to impose upon your loved one the identity of your twin soul. Such a label can become so highly charged with unrealistic expectations that no human can be expected to meet. The pain for you both is then amplified. Likewise let your search for a partner be for the right partner, not just a twin soul. If it is indeed your soul's choice to meet its other half in this life it may need experiences with other partners to prepare you for that experience, just as what a twin soul can bring you is also to prepare you for a greater experience of God.

If you have a special yearning to meet your twin soul then I wish to point you in the direction of your inner partner, the perfect love that is within you now. When a sense of wholeness can follow that fusion you may more easily hope to attract another whole being to you; think of the two wholes coming together as two holes coming together to form the figure of infinity. When you are in perfect resonance with another, as with a twin soul, the love will flow from heart to heart in exactly that configuration.

Think of this: if you have two plants growing in one pot eventually there will not be enough energy in the soil of the one pot to sustain both plants; then either both will die or one will be the stronger but neither will be able to grow as they are meant, to flower and bear fruit. So what does the one who loves plants do? He separates them, perhaps rather painfully because they will have been clinging to each other at the roots in the struggle for survival, and gives to each his own pot, in the soil that is good for the individual plant. They can then grow to their full stature, by drawing upon their own resources and so truly blossom and bear fruit; and the joining together is where the branches lightly touch. But branches grow out in all directions, drawing in energy, so not all will touch the other.

So between two of you, who feel so deeply the love between your souls, be rooted in your relationship to self and the Divine, draw your needs from all around you, not just from that special one. Then you will have a much better chance of coming together in freedom and enjoying a relationship that will be a part of the New Order, where your primary relationship will be with your Source, not with each other; where you will be drawn together principally by a shared higher vision that your souls will make clear to you. Do not look to any other relationship that you have had before or to most of the relationships around you, for you are unlikely to find a role model anywhere for what I mean. You must be pioneers in this.

I know it is what you deeply desire, to find your fellow disciple and go out into the world in your 'twosome'. Whether you do this literally or metaphorically is not important. You can reach right across your planet from the cosy scene in front of the log fire, but if your dream is only that life of cosy domestic bliss then you may be disappointed.

Forgive me for sounding like the stern teacher, but you have work to do. If you feel bored now from not having enough to do I say to you enjoy it while it lasts and prepare for that even greater joy of living your larger purpose.

42

SEXUALITY

YOU KNOW, Dear Ones, far too much suffering is caused to yourselves by yourselves as well as others over the issue of sexuality and sexual orientation.

Let me tell you that we who are your guides and angels working for you on behalf of the Highest are not the slightest bit interested in the plumbing of the person you chose to love. What we are interested in of course is that you do honour and respect the person who you have chosen to love.

The spiritual journey has, as you know, as one of its goals the balance of the masculine and feminine principles within you. Up to now tradition has stated that when a man and a woman come together in sexual union that each can provide the other with the complementary energy. Now that more and more of you are finding a greater balance within yourselves, especially those within a feminine physical body, some of you are being confronted by the unexpected attraction to those in a same gender body. The attraction is not always specifically sexual in nature but energetic. It is the urge towards harmonisation. This is not possible for example for a woman to find in a man who clings rigidly to his masculine polarity.

But an attraction to someone of the same gender is not an indication either of a change in sexual orientation from one to another as if forever shutting a door upon an old self, but should be seen as an extension of possibilities for sharing love and intimacy. It can also be seen as an indication of having reached a point in evolution where you have gone beyond the need to learn anything from one particular orientation or to be confined by labels such as homosexual or heterosexual. Dear Ones, you are not sexuals, you are human beings with all the potentials for a happy and fulfilled life at every level according to your soul's needs which must not be denied because of society's dictates or because being attracted to someone of the same gender does not conform to what you had previously always thought yourself to be or needed to have for your fulfilment.

It is no longer appropriate either to think in terms of sexual union between a man and a woman as being designed for physical procreation only. It will remain the pleasurable task for some, until that is physical conception takes place by thought. But I would ask you to consider what is really meant by your term 'making love' for when two people, regardless of the gender combination but who love each other deeply and resonate with one another in their hearts and souls decide to express that love sexually, that is exactly what they do; they make love, they become a love factory and as their energies merge and especially at the moment of climax love is released into the cosmos as a rose in bloom releases its perfume into the air you breathe.

At this time when so much love is needed in your world the love expressed sexually between two people of any gender combination who consciously offer this fruit of their union to God makes such a gift as precious to your world as any physical procreation. It is to be celebrated, not feared or judged. Love is always good.

I do not want to leave you with the idea either that when you approach that balance of masculine and feminine within you that a sexual relationship with someone of the same gender is either obligatory or inevitable. At such a point of spiritual awareness when you will be wanting only to surrender to God's will in your life, nobody will enter your life by chance but only by a perfect design whose architect is your own soul.

43

Ringing True

THERE WILL be times on your journey when you will find yourself behaving in a way that you will think is inconsistent with the spiritual path. Your shadow will come into sharper focus. Perhaps one person in particular will be pressing your buttons and arousing your life as a gift to you to bring you what you want, which is to grow.

At such times, do not feel ashamed or impatient with yourself or feel that you are failing and letting God down. Remember, there is no judgement! Such behaviour is merely symptomatic of your growing. If you think of a musical scale and you want to go higher from one pure note to another you must pass through discordancy before you hit that higher note.

When you find that you can extend your range to hit that higher note you may decide that you no longer feel comfortable when you descend to those lower vibrations again. Be attentive to the small voice within that tells you that you are not ringing true to the highest in you. It will always be there. It may take quite a few instances of this before you learn to withhold from, shall we say, judgement or criticism of another.

You may then want to look at the reasons why you judge or are critical. Begin affirming 'I now bring to my conscious mind the origin of my need to judge,' or 'I now bring to my conscious mind the origin of my belief that I am wrong.' If you keep saying these while you go about your daily activities, deeply buried memories or impressions may come up to provide the answer.

In time all the parts of you that are unable to ascend the scale must fall away or be removed, but often it will not be without a fight, for the parts which resist will be components of your saboteur that wish to stay alive. If you search hard enough you will find within you aspects that have a vested interest in you staying just as you are. It may be the fear of what you will have to let go of, especially people in your life; it may be fear or ridicule as you embrace openly what you now truly believe; it may be attachment to a persona that has served you well and brought you many rewards at the level of your ego; it may be a prejudice that runs deep, too deep and comfortable to be teased out and convinced of its inappropriateness by any spiritual teaching; it may be an old resentment that you harbour with a certain satisfaction for to let go of it would mean really having to open your heart where you would prefer not to; it may be the habitual belief in being of no consequence as a way to deny your light. Such a habit becomes you about as much as picking your nose in public does.

No Dear Ones, if you are serious about ascending the scale, they all must pass away for they cannot survive the higher vibrations any more than a tree which thrives in the valley floor will bear you fruit when transplanted to the mountain top.

I so much want to impress upon you also, my friends, that there is no great rush for this. Some of you are just too eager to be a saint while you are still alive and therefore risk getting a bad dose of spiritual altitude sickness, thus rendering you incapable of truly helping anyone; you will only be going through the motions of spiritual learning and your spirituality will only be in your head. It is not your will alone that brings about your growth but your intention harmonises itself with the resources of Universal energy as they become more powerfully available to you, just as the potential within an acorn harmonises itself with the elements within the earth, the air and the sun to become that oak tree. Sometimes the conditions for growth are better than others. There are stages too that you have to follow in the right order. The bearing of fruit, the chance to fulfil your largest purpose for which you are most impatient, is usually the last! And all the time you are totally and unconditionally loved by us just as you are.

So we come back once again to the all important factor of your intention and your heart's desire to ring true to it. Let me leave you with this metaphor.

There is a singer and a song, but the song is in a key that is too low for the voice. When the singer tries to sing it, justice cannot be done either to the song or the voice. So what happens is that the song is transposed up to the appropriate key for the voice. The full beauty of both the song and the voice can then be heard and celebrated.

Dear Ones, the song is your personality, the voice is your True Self. The transposer is your soul's intention to realise that point of resonance with the highest in you that only the purest note of love may emerge from you.

After this, singing in the bath will never quite be the same again!

44

YOUR
CHRIST BODIES

IF SOMEONE were to tell you that one day you will be able to travel around your planet without using any form of transport, not even a magic carpet, you would be astounded I am sure. You might be even more astounded when I tell you that you will be able to be in more than one place at the same time as well. It is a possibility for many and for some it is already a reality although they might not be aware of it.

Dear Ones, you are more than just the conscious human being that you see in the mirror. You are aware too that you have a Higher Self but there is a part of you that when you have reached a certain level becomes activated and which can work independently of your normal awareness.

If you look at yourselves now you will find that you are very different to when you took your first steps on your spiritual path. If you had reacted according to the highest in you then in any given situation it would probably not be the way that you would react now, knowing what you now know. Your Higher Self is like a moveable ceiling; as you grow, it gets higher, until resonating with the highest in you reveals a very different you to the one that took their first steps on your journey. But it can only go so high before it activates parts of you that I will call your Christ Bodies.

A Christ Body can appear to someone else as tangible and solid as any ordinary physical presence but it also works invisibly. A Christ Body responds to a call for help; as it answers that call you may feel a split second of dizziness or feel a sudden need to lie down and sleep at an unusual time for you. It is the Good Samaritan that appears out of nowhere in a moment of great need and disappears as quickly or the person in that chance meeting that can offer vital information at the perfect time.

Working invisibly it is the beautiful Being that accompanies a soul newly released from its body to the light, perhaps as a result of an accident, or the visitor in a dream that brings a healing message. Other times it will be seen by yourself or one gifted with spiritual vision as a light Being standing very close to you who you will think is your guide. Of course it is vibrating at a level that frees it from the confines of time and space and can travel to any part of your planet so the next time you are visiting another land and meet someone who you recognise but know you cannot have met, it may not simply be that they remind you of someone but possibly they travelled to you already in a Christ Body.

The reason that you will always remain largely unaware of these activities is that if you know all that you get up to beyond your conscious awareness your ego would find it very difficult to integrate and such work can only take place in the first place when your ego is beyond being massaged by the size or seeming importance of the task you perform.

We might also have to order for you a pair of lead boots!

45

Watch
Your Thoughts

I WANT to tell you a story. Once upon a time there was a set of twins who in their childhood experienced a terrible, terrible trauma which created a pain in them that they had no way of healing.

As they got older one of the twins internalised his pain and fell ill with cancer. Immediately his friends rallied around him and prayed for him. The best medical attention was on hand to try to cure him and everyone felt terribly sorry for him.

The other twin externalised his pain and beat someone up in a fit of rage and his friends rejected him and everyone thought what a terrible man he was. The best legal experience was on hand to make sure that he was punished and sent to jail.

But the root cause of the cancer and the attack was the same pain. The only difference was that the first twin committed a violent act against himself and the second twin against another. Both are equally deserving of compassion and healing. Neither should be judged. If these twins had been brought before Jesus, do you think He would have only healed the one who was ill with cancer? Of course not. Jesus would have healed the wound that gave rise to each ones suffering and the cancer and the rage would have been healed with it.

Not all acts of violence against another arise from a wound in the one who carries out the act; sometimes the violent person has drawn into him or her aggressive thoughts from all around him and acts them out.

Of course you would say that you could never, ever harm anyone but if you have ever had an angry or aggressive thought towards someone then that thought has gone out into the atmosphere, ready for some wounded being to draw it into them and do your dirty work for you. Indirectly you have at least contributed towards someone being harmed. And then when someone has been arrested for some terrible crime another wave of hatred and negativity is released into the cosmos, only fuelling that resource to allow something even more terrible to take place. And so on and so on. The result is that more and more shocking crimes will take place to challenge mankind's resolve not to judge and to respond only with healing love! And as soon as the time comes when more people are sending healing thoughts to those who commit harm against another or against any part of Divine Creation than those who are sending vengeful or judging thoughts, your crime rates will begin to reduce, more trees will be planted than are cut down, the list of endangered species will get smaller, peace will come to war zones. You will see for yourselves the absolute truth in the law of 'As within, so without.'

From now on where once you might have judged or condemned let your knee-jerk response be to ask yourself 'What would Jesus do in this situation?' and the answer will come from the Christ in you. Then you must act on it, for to act in a way that is less than what you know to be true is the greatest crime of all. It may mean having to stick your head above the parapet and putting yourself in the firing line of those who cling together to find safety in masses but to lack the courage to do so is to shoot yourself in the foot and injure your soul. At such a time always remember the words 'if God is for you, what can be against you?'

You do not come into this world as a member of the Vanguard Army to go AWOL at the first opportunity to reveal yourself as a warrior of light. It is at such times that you should remember the saying also 'many are called but few are chosen'. Reacting according to the highest in you and not your fear may be a deciding factor whether you are chosen or not.

46

How You
Can Help

What is the best anyone can do to help our planet at the moment?

THE BEST you can do is to withhold from any judgement about what is taking place and to hold constantly in your mind the vision of your planet as whole and healed.

To be able to do this you need to be able to heal yourselves too because the vision you hold for your planet can only manifest when that vision corresponds with your own state of being.

Let me take as an example your concerns for the pollution affecting your world. Before you are going to be able to cleanse your oceans and rivers and the air you breathe, you need to be able to cleanse the toxicity of thought that surrounds your planet. If you had the eyes to see you would not just see the physical clouds in the sky that from time to time block out the sun and precipitate rain upon the earth, but you would also see the dark clouds of fear, of anger, of hatred that also block out the light of the cosmic sun and which in their own way precipitate those same energies into the consciousness of man. Like the cycle of the rain and the clouds passing between earth and the skies, so the same cycle continues with such thoughts, every bit as destructive as acid rain. So you have those clouds of anger and hatred precipitating those thoughts into those who are already vulnerable; they then act them out, you fear and judge their actions which creates only more negative thoughts to be absorbed back into those clouds.

So begin by working to dissolve that pollution, working with all the love of your heart and all the will of your mind to clear those clouds, some of which you will have created, so that the light of Truth can shine through and all can bask in that light in the same way that on a grey winters day you long to bask in the light and warmth of your physical sun. Get together with two or three people who share that intention, and for as long as you can hold that vision. When you are together imagine yourselves as a link in a chain of all the other small gatherings taking place at the same time with the same intention.

Is that going to stop the destruction of the rain-forests though?

Those who are involved in such acts do not know what they are doing. Attacking them with your thoughts is not going to make them stop what they are doing but risks fuelling their determination to keep on. They are acting out of ignorance and fear and are needing your forgiveness, which is not to say that you acknowledge that what they are doing is wrong and you let them off the hook. It is to understand that they, like you, are essentially innocent. It is also possible that in some perverse way they are making an important contribution towards stopping all harm to your environment. Every tree that is cut down sees one more brick being removed from the walls that separate one nation from another. One factor that all mankind shares is that he inhabits the same planet. Nobody seriously wants to see the destruction of humanity; maybe the risk of that happening has to get so real that suddenly all wars and disagreements will disappear and all will be focussed upon that one glorious attention of loving your beautiful planet. In the meantime, keep holding the vision, keep up the lobbying, continue the education and wherever and whenever you can, offer the more beautiful alternative.

What about wars? How should we respond to what is happening in Yugoslavia now?

Again do not judge. You only see what is happening at the level of human interaction, not what is taking place between souls. Judgement and compassion cannot go hand in hand; what those who may be suffering in a war or famine need is compassion.

In the case of Yugoslavia an old wound has been opened that was closed prematurely, leaving the dirt in it. As with a wound in your physical body, if it is not cleansed it will fester and the pain will get worse, requiring more radical treatment. Perhaps a poultice will be required to draw the poison to the surface. Love is also like a poultice, bringing to the surface anything unlike itself, and it works no less effectively between nations than it does in a relationship between two people. So in Yugoslavia as in many other areas of conflict rest assured that at this time the powers of light and love are working to bring healing, drawing together in a perfect way those whose evolution can be assisted or whose karma can be resolved by being in that situation. Remember, you have been there too in your previous lives and look where you are now, motivated towards creating harmony and peace within yourselves and amongst your fellow men? And when you were in situations of conflict in the past, you chose that too for your evolution. Do not try to understand why a soul would want to enter into a life of suffering in a war or famine; it's none of your business anyway. Your business is to learn how to activate your heart in response to their suffering and to be guided forward through all of life's difficulties by the wisdom contained therein.

The best that any individual can do to make a contribution towards peace anywhere is not to seek it at any price or by forcing those involved to drop their weapons in a negotiated peace because the resentment will remain like the dirt in the wound. By holding the vision of peace you encourage the dirt in the wound to surface and be cleaned away. More than that offer up your love to the Highest, in the same way you might send a donation to a relief organisation, trusting that your money would be spent in a good way. So, trust that the Highest will use your love in a way that will bring lasting good.

There is one more important lesson to be learned by all who are using war or rebellion to gain freedom. When the warring parties in Yugoslavia have found a peace through establishing their autonomy from each other they will believe themselves to be free, just as the people of Eastern Europe believed that the overthrowing of communist régimes would set them free. And yes they gained religious freedom, political freedom and for some even economic freedom; but what they are already discovering is that they are no freer now than they were in the days of communist rule. True freedom does not come with the ballot box or money in your purse or the communion wafer; the power still remains outside of you, with the politicians, or the employer or the priest. True freedom comes with the experience of the Christed heart, and that begins with the overthrowing of all those erroneous beliefs in separation and imperfection and lack that control your life. But first there has to be the experience that what you thought would set you free does not do so. It is no use telling someone who has never had money that money does not make you happy. He wants to find out for himself.

Of course all the changes taking place in your political map have come about as a part of the unavoidable steps that mankind is making towards the establishment of perfect order on Earth. I leave with you the image of a weather map, with all the lines and squiggles on it. At this time a warm weather front is passing through your part of the Cosmos, bringing freedom; behind it are more weather fronts, each bringing the right conditions for the breaking down of the old and the creation of the new. For some it may mean they will have to weather heavy storms in their lives and they will discover that their 'houses' are built on sand, not rock. Those houses may be political ideologies or religious beliefs or too many attachments to that which is transient. Whatever, all will be washed away until every being is living on a foundation of Truth. The Truth, and only the Truth, will set you free. And take courage because throughout all the change you will be perfectly supported and guided and cared for. The loving arms of your Divine Parents are forever poised to catch you when you might fall, just like any parent is there when their child takes its first steps.

Take courage also, Dear Ones, from the words of the Master Jesus 'In this world you have much fear and tribulation; but be of good cheer, for I have overcome the world!'

Stick that on your refrigerator door!

47

THE MESSAGE
OF THE BELOVÉD

THERE ONCE lived upon your planet a great teacher whose name will forever be synonymous with Love. He it was who was closest amongst the first disciples to the Master, the Belovéd One who at the Last Supper rested his head upon the Master's shoulder. It was he who wept with the Mother at the foot of the cross and into whose loving care the Master entrusted the Mother.

And it was he who through his closeness to the Master had been witness to countless miracles and healings and had been present when the teachings you love so well were first given. He heard and saw it all.

And in his old age, for he was the only one of those first twelve disciples who did not die a martyr's death, it was he who received and channelled the vision of the Apocalypse which you call the Revelations.

And having heard and seen and done all that, he did not then start running Apocalypse workshops or teaching how to perform miracles. He did not busy himself on any lecture circuit entertaining people with his reminiscences of his life with Jesus. After all that he was able to distil everything that he knew and had learnt down to three words only. In fact in the closing years of his life they were the only words that ever passed his lips. He would walk the streets of where he lived, supported by his closest disciples, uttering these three words only, the only words that mattered. And these words were...

Love One Another!

48

BLESSING OF
WHITE BULL

AND SO sadly the time has come when I must leave you.

I do so with much love, not only from myself but also from all of those in the World of Light who in any way touch and affect your lives.

We are many, but we are one spirit only in our unceasing prayers for you, for the healing of all that stands between you and your perfect good.

To that end we hold a vision for you, a vision of what you truly are until you can realise it for yourself, sure in the knowledge that filled with the radiance of your own Christ Self you will then experience a life of deep and lasting peace, of great and infinite joy, of perfect and eternal Love.

With all love to you, Dear Ones, I say

God Be With You.

ACKNOWLEDGMENTS

THIS BOOK HAS COME into being through grace and magic. As White Bull might say, God's fingerprints are all over it!

I had known for some time that there would one day be a book of White Bull's teachings but when I knew I had to begin I could only cast my eyes heavenward and remind White Bull that I had nothing to write it on! Within a week my friend Anna De Schutter arrived at the place where I was staying and, out of the blue, gave me a laptop computer.

That was just the beginning. If ever I needed the proof that this was a book that needed to be written I received it in the perfect timing of each gift of energy in all its forms that facilitated the next step in bringing it into your hands now. It also proves the truth expressed in the title.

My most loving thanks go to all of those who have been a part of this magic and grace, who by giving so generously of their love, energy and time to me during the creation of this book have made it all possible. Especially I want to thank Peter Heraty, Donald Pell, Anna De Schutter, Irene Van Lippe-Biesterfeld, Willem and Melanie Renes, Kern Consult bv, Joop and Jeanette Noorlander, Edgar Hoffman, Ann West, André Passé, Lucia Potthoff, Eric Van Der Geest and Herbie Brennan.

I would also like to express my gratitude to all of those who during the last sixteen years have enabled my work with White Bull to happen by opening their hearts and homes to me and all who want to meet White Bull. They are Virginia Arnold, Susan Dunkley, Thierry and Bernadette Van Genebeek, Peter and Bernadette De Ridder, Peter and Neeltje Bollen, Geert Byttebier, Mia Goethals, Nico and Yvonne Bulder, Holly Hilton, Eugenie Heraty, Joop and Reini Bels and Willem and Melanie Renes.

I am especially indebted to my cousin, Tessa Graham, who brought me into contact with The Tagman Press. I am no less indebted to Anthony Grey for his belief in this book and his desire to make the love and wisdom of White Bull available to the English speaking world.

For their unfailing encouragement and moral support during the writing of the book my loving thanks go to my soul sisters Deborah Sabine and Fiona Macniven. And for his contribution to my life during the period of writing, and still today, which only one of the same soul essence could possibly make I thank with all my heart Frans Van Haarlem.

Ian Graham
Normandy, France.
Autumn 2000